The
Teton Sioux ◀Indians▶ ◀of North▶ ◀America▶

DATE DUE

Heritage Edition

◀ **Indians** ▶
◀ **of North** ▶
◀ **America** ▶

Heritage Edition

Indians
of North
America

The
Teton Sioux

Nancy Bonvillain

Foreword by
Ada E. Deer
University of Wisconsin-Madison

CHELSEA HOUSE
PUBLISHERS
A Haights Cross Communications Company

Philadelphia

COVER: A Lakota doll made of beadwork and buckskin.

CHELSEA HOUSE PUBLISHERS

VP, NEW PRODUCT DEVELOPMENT Sally Cheney
DIRECTOR OF PRODUCTION Kim Shinners
CREATIVE MANAGER Takeshi Takahashi
MANUFACTURING MANAGER Diann Grasse

Staff for THE TETON SIOUX

EXECUTIVE EDITOR Lee Marcott
EDITOR Christian Green
PRODUCTION EDITOR Noelle Nardone
PHOTO EDITOR Sarah Bloom
SERIES AND COVER DESIGNER Keith Trego
LAYOUT 21st Century Publishing and Communications, Inc.

A Haights Cross Communications ⭐ Company

www.chelseahouse.com

First Printing

9 8 7 6 5 4 3 2 1

Library of Congress Cataloging-in-Publication Data

Bonvillain, Nancy.
  The Teton Sioux/Nancy Bonvillain.
    p. cm.—(Indians of North America, revised)
Includes bibliographical references and index.
  ISBN 0-7910-7992-9 — ISBN 0-7910-8353-5 (pbk.)
  1. Teton Indians. I. Title. II. Series.
E99.T34B66 2004
978.004'9752—dc22

                                                    2004004705

Contents

Foreword

Ada E. Deer

American Indians are an integral part of our nation's life and history. Yet most Americans think of their Indian neighbors as stereotypes; they are woefully uninformed about them as fellow humans. They know little about the history, culture, and contributions of Native people. In this new millennium, it is essential for every American to know, understand, and share in our common heritage. The Cherokee teacher, the Mohawk steelworker, and the Ojibwe writer all express their tribal heritage while living in mainstream America.

The revised INDIANS OF NORTH AMERICA series, which focuses on some of the continent's larger tribes, provides the reader with an accurate perspective that will better equip him/her to live and work in today's world. Each tribe has a unique history and culture, and knowledge of individual tribes is essential to understanding the Indian experience.

Prior to the arrival of Columbus in 1492, scholars estimate the Native population north of the Rio Grande ranged from seven to twenty-five million people who spoke more than three hundred different languages. It has been estimated that ninety percent of the Native population was wiped out by disease, war, relocation, and starvation. Today there are more than 567 tribes, which have a total population of more than two million. When Columbus arrived in the Bahamas, the Arawak Indians greeted him with gifts, friendship, and hospitality. He noted their ignorance of guns and swords and wrote they could easily be overtaken with fifty men and made to do whatever he wished. This unresolved clash in perspectives continues to this day.

A holistic view recognizing the connections of all people, the land, and animals pervades the life and thinking of Native people. These core values—respect for each other and all living things; honoring the elders; caring, sharing, and living in balance with nature; and using not abusing the land and its resources—have sustained Native people for thousands of years.

American Indians are recognized in the U.S. Constitution. They are the only group in this country who has a distinctive *political* relationship with the federal government. This relationship is based on the U.S. Constitution, treaties, court decisions, and attorney-general opinions. Through the treaty process, millions of acres of land were ceded *to* the U.S. government *by* the tribes. In return, the United States agreed to provide protection, health care, education, and other services. All 377 treaties were broken by the United States. Yet treaties are the supreme law of the land as stated in the U.S. Constitution and are still valid. Treaties made more than one hundred years ago uphold tribal rights to hunt, fish, and gather.

Since 1778, when the first treaty was signed with the Lenni-Lenape, tribal sovereignty has been recognized and a government-to-government relationship was established. This concept of tribal power and authority has continuously been misunderstood by the general public and undermined by the states. In a series of court decisions in the 1830s, Chief Justice John Marshall described tribes as "domestic dependent nations." This status is not easily understood by most people and is rejected by state governments who often ignore and/or challenge tribal sovereignty. Sadly, many individual Indians and tribal governments do not understand the powers and limitations of tribal sovereignty. An overarching fact is that Congress has plenary, or absolute, power over Indians and can exercise this sweeping power at any time. Thus, sovereignty is tenuous.

Since the July 8, 1970, message President Richard Nixon issued to Congress in which he emphasized "self-determination without termination," tribes have re-emerged and have utilized the opportunities presented by the passage of major legislation such as the American Indian Tribal College Act (1971), Indian Education Act (1972), Indian Education and Self-Determination Act (1975), American Indian Health Care Improvement Act (1976), Indian Child Welfare Act (1978), American Indian Religious Freedom Act (1978), Indian Gaming Regulatory Act (1988), and Native American Graves Preservation and Repatriation Act (1990). Each of these laws has enabled tribes to exercise many facets of their sovereignty and consequently has resulted in many clashes and controversies with the states and the general public. However, tribes now have more access to and can afford attorneys to protect their rights and assets.

Under provisions of these laws, many Indian tribes reclaimed power over their children's education with the establishment of tribal schools and thirty-one tribal colleges. Many Indian children have been rescued from the foster-care system. More tribal people are freely practicing their traditional religions. Tribes with gaming revenue have raised their standard of living with improved housing, schools, health clinics, and other benefits. Ancestors' bones have been reclaimed and properly buried. All of these laws affect and involve the federal, state, and local governments as well as individual citizens.

Tribes are no longer people of the past. They are major players in today's economic and political arenas; contributing millions of dollars to the states under the gaming compacts and supporting political candidates. Each of the tribes in INDIANS OF NORTH AMERICA demonstrates remarkable endurance, strength, and adaptability. They are buying land, teaching their language and culture, and creating and expanding their economic base, while developing their people and making decisions for future generations. Tribes will continue to exist, survive, and thrive.

Ada E. Deer
University of Wisconsin-Madison
June 2004

1

The Setting

The Teton (TEE-ton) people once inhabited a vast territory in the northern prairies and plains of North America in the present-day states of Minnesota, North and South Dakota, Nebraska, and Wyoming. Today, most Tetons live in or near *reservation* communities within the region of their traditional lands.

The Teton *tribe* is one of seven divisions, or tribal groups, of American Indians known collectively as the Sioux or the Lakota. The name *Sioux* comes from the language of the nearby Chippewa tribe, who used their word *Nadoweisiweg*, which means "Lesser Snakes," to label their neighbors. When, in the seventeenth century, French traders heard the Chippewa word, they shortened it to *Sioux*. The people call themselves *Lakota*, meaning "allies" or "friends." In some *dialects*, the word is pronounced with a *d* as *Dakota*, from which the states of North and South Dakota get their name.

The Teton *band* is the westernmost Lakota division. The name *Teton* comes from the Native word *tetonwan*, meaning "dwellers of the prairie." The six other Lakota divisions can be grouped into a northern and an eastern section. The northern peoples are called the Yankton, from the Native word *ihanktunwan*, meaning "dwellers of the end." This group consists of the Yankton and the Yanktonai, or the "little Yankton." The eastern peoples are called the Santee Lakota, a term derived from the word *isanti*, meaning "knife." The name comes from the area they inhabited near Knife Lake in present-day Minnesota. The Santees consist of four bands, named the Wahpeton ("dwellers among the leaves"), Mdewakanton ("people of Spirit Lake"), Wahpekute ("shooters among the leaves"), and the Sisseton ("camping among the swamps").

The seven Lakota divisions refer to themselves collectively as members of the Seven Council Fires. They are distinct social and political entities, but they recognize a common *culture* and heritage. They speak separate dialects of the Lakota language and share most characteristics of history, economy, social systems, and religious beliefs. Members of the Seven Council Fires were never integrated into a fixed political structure or confederacy, but they all agreed never to fight one another. They often had common interests and helped each other in times of need.

Of all the Lakota divisions, the Tetons are the most numerous. A number of bands comprise the Tetons. The largest group is the *Oglala*, a name meaning "they scatter their own." Next in size is the *Sicangu* or "burnt thighs." This group is sometimes referred to today as the *Brulé*, from the French word meaning "burnt." The other five Teton bands are called the *Hunkpapa* ("those who camp at the entrance"), *Sihasapa* ("blackfeet"), *Itazipco* ("without bows"), *Oohenonpa* ("two kettles"), and *Miniconjou* ("those who plant by the stream").

Of all these separate names, only the derivation of the *Sicangu* or "burnt thighs" has been convincingly documented. According to the people themselves, an event that occurred in the winter of 1762–1763 gave them their name. In the words of historian George Hyde: "The band was encamped on the shore of a long, narrow lake in eastern South Dakota. The grass of the prairie caught fire. A man, his wife, and some children, who were out on the prairie, were burned to death; the rest of the Sioux saved themselves by leaping into the lake; but most of the Indians had their legs and thighs badly burnt, and scars resulted. The band was therefore given the new name of 'Sichangu' or 'Burnt Thighs.'"

The name tetonwan well describes the original territory of this people. They inhabited the prairies of North America for hundreds of years, living in what is now central Minnesota. They built their villages along the eastern banks of the Missouri River and in the upper valleys of the Minnesota River. In the rich fields, Teton women planted gardens of corn, beans, and squash. They supplemented these foods by gathering wild rice, roots, tubers, and fruits. Teton men hunted animals that roamed the prairies and forests nearby. They especially prized the buffalo, which migrated across the prairies in huge herds, but they also hunted deer and elk in the woods.

In addition to procuring their own resources by farming, hunting, and gathering wild plants, the Tetons traded with neighboring peoples for other goods. Nearby lived Native peoples known as the Arikaras and the Mandans, who planted larger fields than did the Tetons and usually produced a surplus of food. The Tetons often traded with them, obtaining farm crops. In return, the Tetons gave their neighbors animal meat and the hides of buffalo, deer, and elk.

By the seventeenth century, the Lakotas, Arikaras, and Mandans had very distinct cultures, but at some time in the past their ways of life may have been more similar. Evidence of the common ancestry of these peoples comes from the study of their languages. Each group now speaks its own distinct language, but their languages all belong to a family

An 1852 engraving of a Lakota encampment. The *tetonwan*, or "dwellers of the prairie," originally resided along the eastern banks of the Missouri and Minnesota Rivers but moved west in the mid-eighteenth century due to the influx of displaced Indians from the East and European traders and soldiers.

that modern linguists call the Siouan family. Siouan languages share many characteristics of sounds, grammar, and vocabulary. The current languages may have descended from a common language spoken thousands of years ago by ancestors of modern Siouan peoples.

The Tetons continued to live on the prairies of Minnesota until the middle of the eighteenth century. By that time, far reaching changes had occurred in North America—changes that came to have a critical influence on the lives of not only the Lakotas but of all American Indian peoples of the continent.

Fundamental changes in Native American societies were set in motion by the arrival of Europeans on the shores of North America. At first, Europeans were few in number and of little consequence, but their impact on indigenous peoples grew steadily. By the middle of the seventeenth century, many changes in Native life were already taking place. Of utmost importance was the dislocation of American Indians from their ancestral territories as the result of the presence of Europeans. This process began among peoples who originally lived near the Atlantic coast and in nearby inland areas. Many people were killed in attacks by Europeans who wanted to take land for their own settlements. Others were killed in intertribal wars resulting from competition among American Indians for the remaining land and resources.

Still others, probably the greatest number, died from many devastating diseases that swept through Native villages after the Europeans' arrival. These deaths were caused mostly by epidemics of smallpox and measles. Before contact with Europeans, the microorganisms that cause smallpox and measles were unknown in North America. Since the germs did not exist in American Indian communities, the people had never developed immunity to them. When Europeans arrived, carrying these deadly organisms, Native Americans had no natural protection. As a consequence, disease spread with sudden and horrifying swiftness. In many instances, whole families and even entire villages became sick and died. Even those people who survived were often left weak and frightened.

As a result of the combination of European expansion, increased warfare, and disease, American Indians in eastern North America saw their lands diminished in size and their lives changed forever. Some continued to reside in a small portion of their ancestral homelands, but many others decided to leave the area, hoping to find peace and prosperity farther west. However, western lands were occupied by other Native peoples, so a steady process of westward movement and relocation of numerous groups continued for many years.

These events created the setting in which the Tetons found themselves by the eighteenth century. As the pressures resulting

The Black Hills, which the Tetons call *Pahasapa*, stretch across western South Dakota, northeastern Wyoming, and southeastern Montana. The land is sacred to the Tetons and they have been striving to reclaim it from the U.S. government since 1877.

from the dislocation of eastern peoples increased, the Lakotas decided to leave their villages on the prairies. They were reacting to the presence of new American Indian groups who entered the prairies, and of French and British traders and soldiers who made their way into the area.

The Tetons were the first of the Lakotas to cross the Missouri River, heading west onto the Great Plains sometime around

1750. They migrated into present-day South Dakota, reaching the Black Hills by 1765. The Tetons continued to interact with other bands of Lakotas, who soon followed them onto the plains. They also continued to trade with the Arikaras and Mandans, making periodic trading expeditions with these people, who remained in their villages east of the Missouri River.

Once on the plains, the Tetons came into contact with other peoples who resided in the area, including the Cheyennes, Pawnees, Arapahos, and Crows. Some, like the Pawnees, were farmers living in settled villages. Others, such as the Cheyennes and Crows, were *nomadic* and obtained their food from hunting and gathering wild plants.

On the plains, the Tetons gave up their farming economy and their settled village life. Instead they became nomadic, establishing temporary camps and small villages. Over the course of the next one hundred years, the Tetons developed a distinct and thriving culture that grew out of their new circumstances. They adapted to their environment and to an altered way of life. Although this new way required different skills, the Tetons met the challenge of change and prospered during this critical period.

2

Teton Ways of Living

T eton culture of the eighteenth century combined traditional practices and new ways of living. After the Tetons migrated into the Great Plains, they adapted their traditional knowledge and skills to suit their new surroundings. They also adopted new ways of doing things as the need and opportunity arose.

Perhaps the most important innovation in Teton culture was the incorporation of horses into their economy. Ancient species of horses had existed in North America many thousands of years ago, but they became extinct long before the ancestors of American Indians arrived on the continent. Thousands of years later, modern horses were brought to North America by Europeans. The Tetons, like other American Indians living on the open plains, immediately realized the enormous potential for travel and transport that horses (*sunkawakan*) provided. They therefore began to trade for them in large numbers.

When the Tetons crossed the Missouri River around 1750, horses were just beginning to make their appearance on the Northern Plains. Most of these animals were obtained through trading networks originating in the south and the southwest. Native tribes such as the Comanche and Kiowa got horses by trading with or raiding Spanish settlements in present-day Texas and New Mexico. Other American Indians traded with the Comanches to obtain horses. Several tribes, such as the Cheyenne, became middlemen to more northerly peoples, including the Teton. Although the Tetons valued horses highly, they did not acquire as many as some plains groups, as the climate in the region limited the number of horses the Tetons could maintain. Since Teton territory was located in the Northern Plains, winters were extremely cold and it was difficult to find enough grass for horses to eat during the long winter months.

In a short period of time, the use of horses revolutionized the economies of all plains peoples, including the Teton. The Tetons emphasized hunting buffalo (*tatanka*) as their primary means of subsistence. Travel by horseback allowed hunters to go farther from their camps in order to locate the migrating herds. By using horses to carry meat and hides back to camp, men could make more efficient use of their time and effort by killing more buffalo during a single hunting expedition. In the centuries prior to acquiring horses, the Tetons had used dogs to carry loads, but horses could obviously carry and pull much heavier burdens. As an indication of the importance the Tetons gave to horses, the term for these animals was *sunka wakan*, an expression meaning "sacred dog."

Teton men used a number of methods for hunting buffalo. In some cases, individual hunters tracked and attacked single animals. Their hunting gear consisted of wooden lances, or bows and arrows tipped with stone arrowheads. In other cases, hunting parties made up of several men traveled and worked together, attacking larger numbers of animals. Finally, in the

With the acquisition of the horse in the mid-eighteenth century, the Tetons became more of a nomadic society that subsisted mostly on the buffalo. Due to its import in helping the Tetons carry larger loads, the horse became known as *sunka wakan,* or "sacred dog."

massive communal buffalo hunts that occurred every summer, hundreds of Teton men united to kill huge numbers of animals.

Several strategies were used in hunting. One tactic involved surrounding a group of buffalo with a circle of small fires lit on the plains grass. The animals were confined within the circle, because they were afraid of crossing over fire. They were then easily killed by the hunters.

Teton hunters also commonly used a method of driving buffalo over the edge of a cliff. In this method, all able-bodied residents of a camp contributed their labor. Women, children, and older men positioned themselves in lines forming a V to surround a herd of buffalo. The open end of the V led toward a cliff. Then hunters drove the herd forward by shouting and making loud noises to frighten the animals. As the buffalo ran, the women and children continued to shout at them from a distance to keep the animals within the V formation. The buffalo blindly plunged over the edge of the cliff. Many died in the fall itself. Others were killed by hunters waiting for them below.

The same basic method was used to drive a herd of buffalo into a corral put up on the plains by forming piles of stone and brush to make an enclosure. Animals stampeding into the corral were easily killed by the waiting hunters.

Once the animals were killed, Teton women had much work to do. First they cut the meat into smaller pieces so that it could be carried back to camp. Some meat was cooked immediately and eaten on that day, but most of it was preserved for later use. Women cut the meat into thin strips and hung it on wooden racks to dry. Afterward, they packed the dried meat into tight bundles and stored it in their homes. When needed for food, the meat was boiled along with wild berries or plants added for variety and flavor. Some of the dried meat was used to make *pemmican*. Pemmican was prepared by pounding the meat into a powder and mixing it with dried berries. These various methods of preserving meat ensured that supplies obtained in one hunting expedition could sustain the people for a long period of time.

Many other aspects of Teton culture demonstrate the people's ability to adapt to their environment and circumstances. Their tools, utensils, and housing were all lightweight and easy to transport. Teton men and women used wood and animal bone in crafting some of their equipment, including many types of hammers, knives, awls, clubs, bows, arrows, and lances.

The Tetons also made much use of animal hides and wood to construct their living quarters. The Tetons resided in structures known as *tipis*. A tipi is a cone-shaped home, rounded at its base and tapered to an open smoke hole at the top. Most tipis were approximately twelve to sixteen feet in diameter at the base. They were large enough to house a family of parents and children and perhaps a few additional relatives.

Teton men and women combined their labor in construct-ing tipis. Women trimmed eight to twelve buffalo skins so that they fit together exactly. Then they sewed the hides together with strong sinew. Meanwhile, men put up a frame made of wooden poles to support the hides. At the top of the tipi, two buffalo skins were loosely hung at the central smoke hole. The flaps could be opened to allow smoke to leave the tipi, or they could be closed to keep out rain, snow, or cold air. The bottom of the tipi was held in place on the ground by stones spaced around the edge of the hides, but, in hot weather, people rolled the bottom skins up so that fresh air could pass into the tipi. When constructing a tipi, space was left open for a doorway, but it was covered with an extra hide that was held in place with pins made of wood or bone when people wanted it closed.

Tipis had few furnishings. People used buffalo hides for seating, bedding, and covers. A hearth was built in the center of the tipi for cooking and heating.

Some men drew paintings on the skins of their tipis. They used natural dyes to make pictographs that recorded important events. Successful hunting expeditions or bravery in warfare were favorite subjects for the paintings.

Despite their size, tipis were lightweight and could be taken apart in a matter of minutes when the Tetons moved to another location. The wooden poles were attached to the back of a horse and the hides were rolled up and placed on the poles.

Many utensils, equipment, and articles of clothing were also made from hides. Some objects were made from buffalo hides, while others were fashioned from the skins of deer or elk. In order to convert hides into useful items, Teton women tanned them to make them soft. In the tanning process, the raw-hide was scraped with a blade made of elk antler to remove all animal flesh and fat. If the women planned to make the skins into clothing or tipis, they removed the animal's hair from the hide. Hair was left on hides used for bedding and covers. Once the hide was cleaned, it was soaked in water until it became pliable. In the final step of tanning, oils and fats were carefully rubbed into the hide to keep it soft.

In addition to using animal skins for tipis and furnishings, Teton women made numerous kinds of containers out of buffalo, deer, and elk hides. Pouches of various sizes held food, clothing, ornaments, and other personal objects.

Prior to their migration onto the Great Plains, Teton women had made earthen pottery, but when the people became nomadic hunters and gatherers, they gave up the art because pottery was too often broken in transport. One of the earlier uses of pottery had been in cooking. Later, Teton women invented a new technique for preparing food. They first dug a pit in the ground, lined it with animal skins, and filled it with water. Then they heated stones on a fire until they were red-hot and placed them in the water. Heat from the stones made the water boil so that food could be cooked. Spoons made of buffalo horns were used for stirring and serving food, but they were not used when eating. Instead, people simply ate with their fingers.

Teton women were responsible for making the articles of clothing worn by all the people. Most items were sewn from soft, tanned skins of deer and elk. Women generally wore knee-length dresses and leggings reaching up to the knee. Men wore sleeveless shirts, *breechcloths*, and leggings that reached well above the knee. In cold or rainy weather, people covered themselves with warm buffalo robes.

Clothing was often decorated, using two different techniques. Men used dyes to paint designs and pictures on their clothing. Women embroidered dresses, shirts, and moccasins with porcupine quills or beadwork. They made geometric designs and brightly colored shapes. A favorite pattern was an embroidered background of blue or white with a design of blue or red.

Men and women wore various kinds of ornaments on their bodies and in their hair. They liked wearing necklaces and armbands of bone or beads. Some people painted or tattooed designs on their face or body. All children had their ears pierced when they were five or six years old. A man generally did the piercing by making a small hole with a bone needle. Then a string of colored beads was worn as an ear ornament.

Most Teton women and men wore their hair in two braids, often intertwined with colored cloth or beads. Older women wore their hair loose on their backs. Some young men preferred a distinctive hairstyle called a *roach*. A man achieved this effect by shaving the sides of his head and allowing the hair in the center to grow. Young men also wore single eagle feathers in their hair. Such emblems were signs of a man's success in war. Older war leaders sometimes wore large feather bonnets on ceremonial occasions.

Most Teton lived in family units that consisted of a married couple and their children. Sometimes a relative of one of the spouses resided with the group if he or she had no other family. Teton people traced their kinship relationship through both their mother's and father's relatives. This is a system called *bilateral descent*. It is the same kind of system familiar to many Americans today.

Even though the Tetons considered themselves related to people through both men and women, relatives on the father's side played a more important role in a person's life. For example, Teton settlements typically consisted of families related through men. After marriage, men tended to remain in the camps of their fathers. Groups of brothers formed the core of settlements after their father died. Women often moved away from their parents after marriage to take up residence in their husbands' camps.

One reason that related men resided in the same camp was that men had to cooperate in several types of activities. Since hunting was often done communally, men depended on each other for aid. Men also went on raids or to war in small groups requiring the cooperation and support of all. The Tetons assumed that relatives worked best together and could depend on each other most. Since work groups usually consisted of men, it was best that related men live in the same camp.

Of course, as in all things, this rule was not always followed. A married couple might decide to live with the wife's family for many reasons. Perhaps the husband had many brothers, while the wife had none. In such a case, the wife's parents might ask the couple to live with them so that they would not be left alone. Perhaps the husband did not get along well with his own relatives and preferred to move away. People were free to follow their own inclinations and to make decisions that best suited them or their families.

Most Teton marriages were arranged by parents for their daughters and sons. The marriage ceremony consisted of an exchange of gifts between the families of the bride and groom. They gave presents to each other to signal their friendship and respect.

Some marriages were not arranged by parents but started instead with the elopement of the couple. A man and woman might have decided on their own that they wanted to marry and just began to live together. If a man was attracted to a particular woman, the man might show his intentions by courting her. He would sit outside her tipi at night, playing a wooden flute and singing songs of love. If the woman was also interested in the man, she might find reasons to walk alone to fetch water or to collect wood so that she might find a moment to speak privately to the man she liked. Although most Teton people had only one spouse, some families consisted of a husband who was married to two or more wives. In these cases, the wives usually were sisters. Men involved in such marriages were often wealthy and influential. They might own many horses and be successful hunters or warriors.

Ideally, Teton marriages lasted for a lifetime, but divorces often occurred, particularly early in a couple's life together. Divorce simply involved a couple's decision to separate.

Sometimes the decision was made jointly, but in other cases, a husband or wife might choose to end the marriage.

The Tetons considered their relatives the most important people in their social world. A great deal of respect was shown between fathers and sons and mothers and daughters. People also tended to show respect to their older siblings. Relations between sisters and brothers were especially formal. Once they reached their teens, brothers and sisters rarely socialized or joked together. People behaved respectfully toward their grand-parents, and grandparents often showered their grandchildren with affection.

Relations between parents-in-law and their children's spouses were very formal. A woman and her son-in-law ideally avoided being in each other's presence and did not speak to each other directly. If they had to be together, they conducted themselves with great decorum. A son-in-law avoided doing or saying anything that might offend his mother-in-law. This type of behavior was a sign of respect and honor.

The lives of the Tetons followed a typical cycle from birth through puberty, adulthood, and death. When a pregnant woman knew she was about to give birth, she stayed in her tipi accompanied by older women who served as midwives. Men were not allowed in the tipi during or soon after delivery. Shortly after birth, the baby was given a personal name by an older male or female relative. As a child grew up, he or she often received additional personal names based on some physical characteristic or personality trait.

When a girl reached puberty, a special ceremony was held for her. During her first menstruation, the girl went to stay for a few days in a hut built for her outside the camp. Older women accompanied her and instructed her about the work and responsibilities of adult Teton women. She was taught how to behave with respect toward others.

Two to three weeks later, the girl's father sponsored a public ceremony and feast to mark the occasion of his daughter's passage to womanhood. The ritual was conducted by a man chosen by the girl's parents. As described by J.R. Walker, a physician who lived among the Oglalas for many years in the early twentieth century, the ritual leader

> painted red the right side of the young woman's forehead and a red stripe at the parting of her hair, and while doing so he said, "You see your oldest sister on the altar. Her forehead is painted red. Red is a sacred color. Your first menstrual flow was red. You have taken of the red water [red chokecherry juice] on this day. This is to show that you are akin to the Buffalo God and are his woman. You are entitled to paint your face in this manner." He then tied the eagle plume at the crown of her head and said, "The spirit of the eagle and the duck are with you. They will give you the influence of the Sun and the South Wind. They will give you many children."

The pubescent girl was given a new set of clothing as a symbol of her adult status and her new role in the community. Relatives and neighbors attended the ceremony to honor the girl and her family.

A boy's passage to manhood was marked when he achieved success in activities typical of Teton men. For instance, when a boy went hunting and killed his first animal, his family gave a public feast in his honor. When he first joined a raiding or war group, his parents held a similar celebration.

Young adults often engaged in a ritual called a *Vision Quest*. They sought visions of a supernatural spirit who would afterward become a personal guardian for them. Although Vision Quests were especially important for men, many women also sought supernatural guardians. Before setting out on the quest, men and women prepared themselves by fasting for four days. At the end of this period, they went through ritual purification in a *sweat bath*. The Teton considered sweats to be sacred events. The act of sweating symbolized shedding of physical and psychological impurities. Sweat baths cleansed people's minds and spirits and prepared them to face the world of supernatural beings.

The Vision Quest itself lasted four days. The seeker left camp alone and proceeded to an isolated place to think and pray for aid. During this period, he or she did not eat or sleep. All the seeker's thoughts and actions focused on encountering a spirit. Seekers offered prayers to the spirit world, asking for guidance. One such prayer, recorded by the great Oglala spiritual leader Black Elk (born in 1863), asks for help for himself and his people:

> Grandfather, I am sending a voice!
> To the Heavens of the universe, I am sending a voice,
> That my people may live!

If the quest was successful, a spirit spoke to the seeker and gave him or her special songs or instructions to follow when in danger or need. Afterward, whenever the seeker was in peril or suffered misfortune, he or she could use these songs and prayers to call on the spirits for help.

People often found distinctive objects during their Vision Quests, which they kept as tokens of their experience. They might find such items as eagle feathers, oddly shaped stones, or animal bones. These tokens took on personal meaning for the seeker. They were put in pouches and kept at home or carried whenever the seeker traveled from camp. (For additional information on this spiritual journey of discovery, enter "Lakota Vision Quest" into any search engine and browse the many sites listed.)

At the end of life, people were expected to face death with courage. But after someone died, relatives went into a period of deep mourning. The deceased's body was placed in the branches of a tree or on a scaffold erected for the purpose. Personal objects of the deceased were usually put with the body to comfort the soul. Offerings of food were also typically placed there so the deceased's soul would have some nourishment as it journeyed away from this world.

Since the Tetons lived in relatively small settlements, they did not develop overarching political structures to govern themselves. Instead, they relied on public opinion to ensure that all people adhered to rules of proper behavior. If someone committed an offense against others, people in the community showed their disapproval by publicly ridiculing the wrongdoer. They might gossip about him within earshot or tease him whenever they met. People faced with such public criticism usually felt ashamed and made sure to correct their behavior in the future.

If conflicts arose between members of the community, they could seek advice from a council composed of elder men in the settlement. These men heard arguments presented by the parties concerned and sought additional information when needed. Their decisions had influence in the community but they had no formal or absolute authority. They could not enforce their judgments but rather relied on public opinion to support them.

Leadership by individuals was relatively weak among the Tetons. Some men were seen as leaders or chiefs, but their position was unstable. A man was respected as a leader based on his success in hunting or warfare. Other desirable traits included intelligence, generosity, even temper, and skill as an orator. Chiefs were admired and respected but they had no authority over others. They could not force anyone to follow their advice or plans. People heard the chief's opinions and then were free to decide for themselves on the proper course of action.

Although most chiefs remained respected members of their community, if they became arrogant or were frequently mistaken in their judgments, people would simply begin to speak ill of them or ignore them. Such men were no longer thought of as leaders. They lost their position in society because of their own behavior.

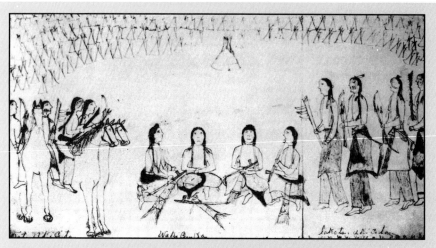

A drawing of a Lakota council. A group of elders comprised the council, which offered advice when conflicts occurred. However, the council had no absolute authority, but instead relied on public opinion to render decisions.

In addition to the older men who functioned as chiefs, some young men were known as war leaders. These men were active and successful in raiding or warfare. They were leaders of military expeditions, but membership in war groups was completely voluntary. A leader could speak to other men and present them with his plans for action, but no one was in any way compelled to join the group. However, if a war leader was usually successful, other men were eager to do as he suggested. Warfare came to play an important role in the lives of Teton men. It was often motivated by a desire to obtain horses in raids against other tribes. As competition for land and resources increased in the nineteenth century, warfare was often necessary as a means of defense against Anglo or American Indian intruders.

Warfare in plains societies had several ritualistic traits as well. Men who wanted to participate had to follow two rules in the days prior to leaving for war. For four days before setting out, they were not allowed to engage in sexual activity. In addition, they underwent ritual purification in a sweat bath.

This act cleansed their bodies and spirits, giving them strength and courage to face dangers encountered in conflict.

Actions in raids or war were judged according to complex rules of bravery. The Tetons, like other plains peoples, had a system of noting war exploits called *counting coup*. In this system, various actions were ranked on the basis of dangers encountered by a warrior. The most prestigious act was to approach an enemy, attack him at close range, and then get away safely. For example, wounding an enemy by clubbing him brought more honor than shooting from a distance because it meant that the warrior had to expose himself to direct danger of retaliation or defeat. Success in face-to-face combat was considered honorable. Other daring actions included wresting a weapon from an enemy's hand or stealing a horse from inside an enemy village.

In addition to civil and war leaders, some Teton men and women gained prestige through their membership in various social groups active in Teton communities. These groups were centered on particular activities. Some were military or ritual societies. Each group had its own songs, dances, and distinctive insignia identifying members. People joined these voluntary groups based on their personal interest and/or selection by members of the group. An invitation to join was made to an interested individual. Then the inductee went through a rite of initiation and presented gifts of thanks to other members.

The most prestigious of the Teton social groups was one named *Heyoka*. Heyoka were men who received their calling through visions from the spirit world. A spirit appeared to a man either in a dream or while awake and told him that he was chosen to become a Heyoka. Once in the group, Heyoka had to do everything in reverse of the normal pattern. They walked backward, sat backward while riding horses, and reversed their clothing. Their actions were both serious and comical to onlookers. This dual role was well explained by the Oglala healer Black Elk in his autobiography. Speaking of the effect of

Heyoka on other people, Black Elk said: "The people shall be made to feel jolly and happy, so that it may be easier for the power to come to them. The truth comes into this world with two faces. One is sad and suffering and the other laughs; but it is the same face, laughing or weeping. When people are already in despair, maybe the laughing face is better for them; and when they feel too good and too sure of being safe, maybe the weeping face is better for them to see."

From time to time, Heyoka men sought visionary contact with spirits in order to strengthen their powers and to receive instruction. A vision seeker fasted and purified himself through a sweat bath. Then he prayed for spiritual aid. Dreams often were important vehicles for contact with spirits. The seeker interpreted episodes depicted in his dreams or he asked other men with spiritual knowledge to determine the meaning of his dreams.

Teton men and women who were thought to have great spiritual powers were among the most respected members of their communities. Many people consulted them, asked their advice, and sought their aid in times of sickness and misfortune. Spiritual leaders were also medical healers. They used many different therapeutic techniques to cure illness. They studied medicinal properties of herbs, tree bark, wild fruits, tubers, and other plants. In addition, healers cured with the aid of spirit guardians whose help they sought in diagnosing the cause of a patient's ailment. Ritual cures often included songs, prayers, and dances aimed at obtaining powers of supernatural forces to cure disease. In addition to their curing abilities, women and men with spiritual powers could foretell future events. They were able to call upon their guardian spirits to receive messages from the supernatural realm.

The supernatural realm of the Tetons was inhabited by many different kinds of spirits. All spirit beings and entities were considered *wakan*, or "sacred." The most important beings were sun (*wi*), sky (*skan*), and earth (*maka*). The sun and sky were endowed with male characteristics whereas the earth was thought of as female. The earth was often called "all-mother" and thus was a symbol of generation, birth, and growth.

Next in importance were spirits of winds, the four cardinal directions of North, South, East, and West, the Thunderers, and spirits of Buffalo and Bear.

A special role in Teton religion was given to a deity called White Buffalo Calf Woman. Her origin is said to have been in the past when there was warfare between human beings and buffalo. After many conflicts, the spirit of Buffalo sent White Buffalo Calf Woman to the people to bring them peace and knowledge. She gave people a Sacred Pipe that they could smoke to send their messages to the supernatural world. The pipe thus creates bonds between inhabitants of natural and spiritual realms of existence. In addition to the gift of the pipe, White Buffalo Calf Woman gave the Tetons seven rituals that form the basis of their religious practice. Of these, the four most important rites include the sweat bath, which is performed to purify people's bodies and minds; the Vision Quest through which people seek visions and aid from spirits; the girl's puberty ceremony; and the *Sun Dance*, performed every summer to give thanks for life, health, and good fortune.

The Sun Dance was a central and dramatic Teton ritual. Sun Dances were held every summer in conjunction with annual buffalo hunts and community social activities. At this time, the separate Teton bands joined together in a large encampment consisting of hundreds of people. Each band had its assigned place in a large circular settlement. The circle was left open toward the east. The Lakota considered the east (*wiyohinyanpata*) to be the most sacred direction since it was the place of the rising sun. The east thus symbolized renewal and growth of the earth and all living creatures. Preparations for a Sun Dance actually began months before the summertime, when a man or woman voluntarily made a vow to sponsor the ritual. An individual might make a vow to sponsor a dance in thanks for recovery from illness or alleviation from some other misfortune. The sponsor first went to a healer and declared his intention. The healer then began to make plans and set a date for the upcoming event.

Four days of preliminary preparation preceded the actual dance. During these four days, a group of men chose a special tree for the central pole of the Sun Dance Lodge. This tree was then considered sacred. Once chosen, the tree was approached by men on horseback and set upon in a mock attack as though it were a prized buffalo.

The Sun Dance itself consisted of various events that were held over the next four days. It began with a procession of men and women to the Sacred Tree. The tree was cut down by a group of women. Then all proceeded to the Sun Dance area and set about constructing the Sun Dance Lodge and installing the tree as the central pole. The pole was decorated with feathers, insignia, and an effigy of the spirit of Buffalo. An altar was erected in the lodge, also dedicated to the spirit of Buffalo.

The most dramatic episode of a Sun Dance occurred on the last day. It centered on the activities of several men who had pledged to participate as dancers. Candidates were expected to embody the moral values of Lakota society, including bravery, generosity, fortitude, and personal integrity. As a mark of their special status, they were given shirts of tanned hide painted red and sets of armbands and anklets. The men prepared themselves for their ordeal by praying to spirits, asking for strength, courage, and good fortune. On the day of the Sun Dance, the dancers rose early, watched the rising sun, and walked in a slow procession to the Sun Dance Lodge. Some of these men had pledged to show their bravery by piercing the flesh on their back and chest with small skewers attached to sinew cords tied to the Sun Dance pole. They sang, prayed, and danced in a circular movement around the Sun Dance Lodge. After many hours, dancers broke free of the cords tying them to the Sun Dance pole, in the process wrenching pieces of skin from their bodies. These acts were considered signs of physical and spiritual daring. Men who engaged in such activity were honored by others in their community.

The Sun Dance ritual drew together all members of the Teton community. It unified them with a common goal of celebrating health and success, and it allowed them to express their gratitude to the spirits for the bounty of the universe. The ritual embodied underlying values of Teton society: the desire for harmony, health, and prosperity and the pledge of cooperation and generosity to one's family and community.

With their ability to transform and adapt their cultural practices and beliefs, the Tetons were set to play an important role in the history of American Indian life in the Great Plains. They successfully met challenges from the new setting in which they found themselves. And for a time, they successfully met challenges brought by settlers from European and American societies in the eighteenth and nineteenth centuries.

3

Meeting the Challenge of Change

During a period of one hundred years beginning in 1750, the Tetons thrived in the Northern Plains region that had become their homeland. They developed a robust economy based on their use of horses to follow herds of buffalo and to transport the increasing amounts of food and goods that the people possessed.

The Tetons also adapted to new neighbors and to the constant flow of intruders into the region. In addition to the Tetons, other American Indians such as the Cheyennes, Arapahos, and Crows were migrating to the plains. The Tetons quickly began to interact and trade with these groups. At first, relations among American Indians living in the plains were generally friendly. But conflicts later erupted among various peoples because of changing circumstances brought about by contact with European and American traders. Trade with European and American merchants first increased the fortunes of American Indians in the plains but then proved to be a cause of conflict in the region.

The Tetons became familiar with goods of European manu-facture through their ongoing trade with American Indians who remained in the eastern prairies. The Mandans and Arikaras living along the Missouri River supplied the Tetons with products obtained in trade with Europeans and Americans. The Tetons especially prized utensils, tools, and weapons made of metal. They traded for knives, nails, needles, kettles, scissors, and arrowheads. Guns and ammunition also became desirable items. In exchange for manufactured goods, the Tetons gave buffalo meat and hides to their trading partners.

Throughout the latter half of the eighteenth century, Teton men and women made yearly trips to present-day Minnesota to trade with the Mandans and Arikaras who obtained European goods from French merchants. The French eagerly expanded their trading networks westward from their original bases in eastern Canada. This trade increased after the French were expelled from the East by the British in 1763 after the French and Indian War.

The Tetons did not deal directly with French merchants because they had already left their lands in the prairies of Minnesota where the French built trading posts. But they were familiar with French products and traders from earlier times. As early as 1682, the Lakotas were visited by a French trader named Pierre Le Sueur. In 1695, Le Sueur persuaded several Lakota leaders to travel to Montreal to meet with traders there. Some trade between the Lakotas and the French continued into the early 1700s while the Lakotas remained in their eastern prairie territory. Later, however, when the Tetons crossed westward into the plains, their dealings with French merchants became indirect. Since the Tetons maintained economic and social relations with other American Indian tribes that remained on the prairies, they obtained French goods through these connections.

An additional source of trade became important to the Tetons in the early nineteenth century. American traders based in St. Louis, Missouri, expanded their businesses by traveling north along the Missouri River. They made direct contact with the Tetons and exchanged American products for animal hides and meat hunted by Teton men and prepared for market by Teton women. Although buffalo hides were the Tetons' major marketable item, they also traded beaver and muskrat to American merchants.

In addition to trading for their own supplies, the Tetons became middlemen between American traders and other American Indians living in the Northern Plains. Their position as go-between meant that Teton traders increased their own wealth and established economic dominance in the region. Indeed, in 1805, the American explorers Meriwether Lewis and William Clark described the Lakotas as the dominant economic and political power along the Missouri River. (For additional information on Lewis and Clark's dealings with the Sioux, enter "Lewis and Clark encounter the Sioux" into any search engine and browse the many sites listed.)

The Tetons traded with merchants from several American companies. Most important was the American Fur Company of St. Louis. The company built a large trading post at the site of present-day Pierre, South Dakota, as well as some smaller stations along the Missouri River. In the 1830s, competitors from the Rocky Mountain Fur Company began to make inroads into Teton territory. In 1834, merchants from the Rocky Mountain Company built their own post on the North Platte River in Wyoming. The trading post, later known as Fort Laramie, became a major commercial center for the Teton region. In addition to the Tetons, the Cheyennes and Arapahos traveled to trade at Fort Laramie.

Although the Tetons and other American Indians greatly desired the implements and weapons they received from Europeans and Americans, trade created unforeseen problems for them. As their familiarity with manufactured goods increased, items that began as novelties and luxuries quickly

Fort Laramie, which was established in 1834, was located on the North Platte River in what is now southeastern Wyoming and served as a trading post for the Teton and other plains tribes.

became necessities in their changing way of life. The people preferred to obtain metal goods rather than spend many long hours making utensils from stone and wood as they previously had done. Not only did their traditional methods require much time to create objects, but the items also broke or wore out more quickly than did goods made of metal. In order to obtain growing amounts of manufactured goods, Teton hunters had to hunt and kill more and more buffalo to give to European and American traders. This need forced Teton men to spend more of their time and energy pursuing buffalo. And Teton women had to spend more of their time and energy processing buffalo meat into dried pemmican and tanning buffalo hides for the market.

By the middle of the nineteenth century, increased trade resulted in depletion of resources in the plains. Buffalo herds became smaller owing to the expansion of hunting made necessary by the needs of trade. Although there were still considerable numbers of buffalo, their decline from previous years created conflict among American Indian peoples over the remaining animals. Conflicts erupted from time to time in warfare and raids of each other's camps. In these attacks, raiders often stole horses from other American Indians. If a man was able to take someone else's horses, he increased his own wealth and ability to travel and transport goods and also decreased his enemy's wealth and freedom of movement.

In addition to economic and technological changes in Teton life directly resulting from trade with Europeans and Americans, some indirect cultural changes also took place. One change involved the way that people regarded themselves and others. Teton society had previously recognized each individual as equal to others. Differences in wealth and status did not exist. In fact, if some people had greater success in hunting than their relatives and neighbors, they customarily shared whatever they had with those in their community who were less skilled or less fortunate. Sharing and generosity were considered extremely important. These norms guaranteed the survival and well-being of all. However, as people amassed horses and goods in large numbers, they began to think of themselves as different based on the amount of possessions they had. Wealth and rank were measured in many ways, especially in numbers of horses that an individual owned. Horses were a sign of wealth and a sign of daring since a man often obtained many of his horses by raiding other peoples.

Another important effect of trade in Teton life was a change in relations between women and men. In traditional times, husbands and wives were generally close in age and status. Although husbands were usually older than their wives, the difference was of only a few years. People typically married when women were in their later teenage years and men in their late teens or early twenties. Then, during the first half of the nineteenth century, Teton norms for marriage changed. People preferred for their daughters to marry men who had already established their reputations as good hunters and warriors. In order for a man to acquire these skills and reputation, he had to delay marriage, often until he was in his thirties.

At the same time, the age when women married was decreasing. Parents often arranged marriages for daughters when the girls were in their early teens. A reason for this change was connected to another change in marriage customs. In traditional Teton culture, most people were married to one mate. But by the nineteenth century, some men were married to more than one woman. Successful and wealthy men some-times married three or four women and thus established large families for themselves. The reason men wanted several wives was that, as a man hunted and killed many buffalo at a time, he needed the help of more women to prepare dried buffalo meat and to tan buffalo hides for trade. A man with more than one wife was in a better position to increase his wealth through trade than was a man with only one wife. And having several wives also meant that a man would have many children. His sons could help him hunt for more buffalo and his daughters could help their mothers prepare buffalo meat and hides.

Teton girls were trained from an early age in the skills of tanning and sewing. They were sought for marriage at a young age by men desiring to expand their wealth. Girls were valued in part because of their ability to process buffalo for the market. A girl was also valued by her father because when she married, her husband customarily gave gifts of horses to the girl's father. Fathers were thus often persuaded to allow their daughters to marry at early ages to men well into their thirties or even beyond.

Finally, as women became increasingly younger than their husbands, their status within their households declined. Age was an important factor in any individual's status. Young people of either gender were expected to be polite and deferential to their elders. Young wives therefore were taught to defer to their husbands.

A further cultural change occurring in the nineteenth century was an increase in the importance of chiefs. The Tetons recognized two different kinds of chiefs: *peace chiefs* and *war chiefs*. Peace chiefs were usually elder men who had proven their abilities as successful hunters when they were in their prime. In addition, they often had religious powers and had visionary contacts with guardian spirits. Many chiefs were also healers and could help people recover from serious illnesses. Peace chiefs were successful in life's experiences and were also men of even temper, great intelligence, and compassion for others. They were generous and shared their wealth with people in need.

War chiefs, on the other hand, were usually young men in the prime of life. They were brave and daring in warfare. They continually proved their ability to lead others in successful raids. Although war chiefs had responsibilities to plan and carry out attacks against their enemies, they were under the general authority of elder peace chiefs.

Since war chiefs were relatively young, they listened to advice from the elder men. In later Teton history, however, young men sometimes were impatient to attack their enemies. Then they acted without the approval of peace chiefs. This change proved to be a disruptive force in Teton community life in the latter half of the nineteenth century.

Disruption of Teton life came from other sources as well. Intrusions into Teton territory by American traders, travelers, and settlers increased throughout the nineteenth century. Populations in eastern states were growing and many eastern farmers heard that there was a large amount of land in the prairies and plains that would be good for cultivation. Many families set out to make new lives for themselves. But the land they came upon was not unused territory. American Indian villages were not located close together—open lands were important to Native peoples. The people used the land for hunting. Each group traditionally controlled a large territory in order to support its community throughout the year. American settlers and the U.S. government did not respect the American Indians' rights to all of their traditional territory. Farmers and ranchers encroached on American Indians' land. In response, Native American peoples tried to defend their territory, resorting to attacks against intruders after negotiations failed to dissuade the settlers. The U.S. government and its army rarely sided with the original inhabitants but instead protected settlers. The army attacked the Tetons and other American Indians who tried to dislodge the American intruders.

The discovery of gold in California in 1848 prompted another large group of American travelers to make their way through the plains. Most of these people were merely temporary nuisances, but others decided to stay and set up farms in the region. Increased encroachments led to intensification of hostilities between Native Americans and intruders. This, in turn, led to expansion of conflict between Natives and the U.S. Army. In numerous raids, the army destroyed many Native settlements and killed thousands of Native people.

Thousands more died from infectious diseases that spread throughout the plains in the nineteenth century. Epidemics of measles and smallpox spread rapidly in Native communities. In a devastating epidemic of smallpox that occurred throughout the plains in 1837, half of the Native population perished. Smallpox, measles, and influenza, all diseases of European origin, brought death in large numbers among American Indian peoples who had never experienced these illnesses and who therefore had no natural immunities or resistances to them. Even survivors were left in a weakened and debilitated condition. They were less able to carry out their normal economic duties or to defend themselves against their enemies.

Another source of foreign intrusion came to the plains in the form of missionary activity. European and American ministers entered the region in the nineteenth century in order to convert American Indians to Christianity. Missionary activity in the area had actually begun two centuries earlier, when a French Jesuit named Father Jacques Marquette first contacted the Lakotas in 1674. Marquette's efforts, however, proved fruitless. Other French missionaries again attempted to convert the Lakotas in the eighteenth century, working among them from 1727 to 1737. These efforts also proved unsuccessful. But when British and American ministers came to the plains in the nineteenth century, they had more success in converting the Lakotas.

Protestant missionaries working for the United Foreign Mission Society established missions among the Lakotas in the 1820s. Presbyterian ministers likewise contacted the Lakotas beginning in 1834. They were followed in the 1850s and 1860s by Roman Catholic missionaries. Although the great majority of Tetons were not swayed by any of these attempts, Christian workers continued their efforts.

In the nineteenth century, the U.S. government decided to proceed with a policy of negotiating treaties with American Indians living in the plains. The government wanted to establish secure zones for settlement. In order to accomplish this goal, they had to force the original inhabitants to give up some of their land. Some Native Americans, including the Tetons, were compelled to surrender their land because they felt they were in a desperate situation. The Tetons hoped that if they agreed to the terms, the U.S. government would protect the land remaining under Teton control. They hoped that American settlers would not be permitted to encroach on more Teton land.

The history of treaties between the Lakotas and the U.S. government began in the early nineteenth century with the signing of treaties of "friendship" between the two groups. The first such document was signed in 1816. It spoke of friendship and peace between the Lakotas and the Americans, expressing lofty pledges. For example, Article I of the *treaty* states that "every injury or act of hostility, committed by one or either of the contracting parties against the other, shall be mutually forgiven and forgot." Article II declares that "there shall be perpetual peace and friendship between all the citizens of the United States, and all the individuals composing the aforesaid tribes [namely the Lakota]." Similar sentiments were expressed in a treaty signed between the Lakotas and the United States in 1825.

Then, in 1837, the Lakotas agreed to formally cede to the United States all the land they had once inhabited east of the Mississippi River. By that year, the Lakotas were no longer living in this territory, since they had all migrated west into the plains. The Treaty of 1837 was thus a formal recognition of their changed life. In exchange for the land, the U.S. government made four promises to the Lakotas. First, it gave the tribe $300,000 as an initial payment. Second, it promised to provide annuities each year consisting of agricultural tools, mechanics' tools, and livestock. Third, the government offered to provide the Lakotas with the services of a physician and a blacksmith. And fourth, it pledged to give an unspecified amount of provisions to the Lakotas for a period of twenty years.

In contrast to treaties signed in the early part of the nineteenth century that essentially established friendship and goodwill between the Lakotas and the United States, treaties of the later years resulted in major losses of land for the Lakotas. The first such treaty, signed in 1851, marked the end of the period of growth and success for Lakota peoples. From that time onward, lands were ceded to the United States. The Teton and other Lakota bands were forced to accept unfavorable terms because of their desire to end brutal attacks against their villages by the U.S. Army and American settlers.

The federal government gave great importance to the Treaty of 1851. It knew that the treaty signaled a change in

Red Cloud (right) and American Horse. Red Cloud (1822–1909) was largely responsible for forcing the U.S. Army to abandon its forts along the Bozeman Trail after leading numerous assaults on the army's garrisons. As a result, the Fort Laramie Treaty was signed in 1868, granting the Tetons control of western South Dakota, including the sacred Black Hills.

power relations between the government and Native peoples. Because of the importance of this treaty, the United States was represented at the negotiations and signing by David Mitchell, then the federal commissioner of Indian affairs. Mitchell headed the *Bureau of Indian Affairs* (BIA), the federal agency established in 1824 to oversee U.S. policies and actions regarding American Indians.

In the Fort Laramie Treaty of 1851, the Lakotas were forced by their circumstances to agree to a reduction in the size of their lands in present-day South Dakota. They managed to retain the territory bounded by the Heart, Missouri, White, and North Platte Rivers. Their title to the Black Hills in western South Dakota was also recognized. But the Tetons lost the major portion of land they had originally controlled. The Tetons also agreed to allow the safe passage of Americans who traveled through their lands heading west. In exchange for land, the Tetons were offered annuities for a period of fifty-five years. Although the terms of the treaty were unfavorable for the Tetons, they were motivated to sign it due to the encroaching American settlements and by the hope that if they agreed to give up some of their land, they would be able to keep the remainder in peace and safety. Unfortunately, such a hope proved unfounded. As the great Lakota leader Red Cloud (1822–1909) later said of the U.S. government: "They made us many promises, more than I can remember, but they never kept but one. They promised to take our land and they took it."

4

The Crisis Continues

Just as the second half of the eighteenth century had been a turning point for the Tetons, the second half of the nineteenth century was also critical in the lives and history of Teton people. In the late eighteenth century, the Tetons had expanded their economies and developed many of their cultural traditions. But in the late nineteenth century, they experienced numerous hardships and disasters. Most of their land was taken by the U.S. government, their traditional livelihood was destroyed, and their freedom of movement was denied. Thousands of Teton died, victims of brutal attacks by the U.S. Army and of devastating epidemic diseases that plagued their communities.

The half century began with the signing of the first treaty of land cession in 1851. Then, during the 1850s and 1860s, warfare in the plains intensified as more American settlers made their way into the territory. The U.S. Army protected settlers and unleashed

38

The signing of the Fort Laramie Treaty, April 1868. The terms of the treaty, which were never upheld, called for the Tetons to have "absolute and undisturbed use" of the area west of the Missouri River in South Dakota and east of the Rockies. In addition, the Bozeman Trail—the major east-west trading route in the area—was to become "unceded Indian territory," i.e., whites weren't permitted to settle there and no U.S. military posts were to be established in the area.

raids against the Tetons and other American Indians who defended their homelands. Major wars erupted in Minnesota, the Dakotas, Nebraska, Kansas, and Colorado. In 1868, as a result of constant turmoil and bloodshed the Tetons agreed to terms of an important treaty signed at Fort Laramie. In it, the Tetons ceded much of the land they controlled in South Dakota. They kept for themselves the territory between the Missouri River in the east, westward to the border of present-day South Dakota and Wyoming. This land, encompassing half of the state of South Dakota, was named the Great Sioux Reservation.

The term reservation (*reserve* in Canada), which is widely used for American Indian land in North America, comes directly from the wording of many treaties between American Indians and the U.S. government. In the treaties, American Indians agreed to cede a specified portion of their original territory and "reserve for themselves" another specified amount of land. A "reservation" therefore consists of the land that the original inhabitants "reserved for themselves." In exchange for land ceded by American Indians to the United States in treaties, the U.S. government pledged to protect Natives' rights to their reservations and to bar outsiders from encroaching on this territory.

In addition to defining the borders of the Great Sioux Reservation, the Treaty of 1868 stated that the U.S. government would give farm animals, equipment, and rations to the Tetons. The government hoped the Tetons would give up their traditional way of life that was based on hunting buffalo in a vast open territory. U.S. officials wanted the Tetons, as well as other American Indians throughout the plains, to become farmers. These officials wanted Indians to adopt the American style of rural living on small farms owned by individual families. They opposed Native traditions which held that all land was controlled by the entire community, not by a single individual. The government also opposed Native practices of traveling from place to place, hunting wild animals and gathering natural vegetation. They wanted American Indians to remain in one place so that they could be more easily supervised and controlled.

In keeping with these goals and in order to entice the Tetons to conform to the officials' plans, the government promised to give twenty-five thousand cows, one thousand bulls, oxen, farming tools, and enough seeds for two years of planting. They also pledged to provide rations of beef, rice, flour, beans, sugar, coffee, and soap.

Finally, the Treaty of 1868 mentioned the existence of "unceded Indian territory" that the Tetons could use. American settlers were barred from encroaching on either the Teton reservation lands or "unceded Indian territory." However, such pledges were soon broken.

When gold was discovered in the Black Hills of South Dakota in 1874, the government began to deny the Tetons rights to their own land. The Black Hills were initially included in the territory possessed by the Tetons as agreed in the Treaty of 1868. The Tetons considered the Black Hills to be sacred land and were determined to keep the region. But the discovery of gold lured many American prospectors, traders, and settlers onto Teton land. Encroachment by Americans obviously violated terms of the treaty. In response to threats posed to Teton peace and survival, Teton warriors defended their communities and attacked the illegal settlements of Americans. And, as in the past, the U.S. government sent armies to protect the violators rather than defend the Native people.

When the U.S. government sent a delegation to the Tetons in 1874 to try to buy the Black Hills for a sum of $6 million, the Tetons refused. Nonetheless, more settlers and prospectors streamed into Teton territory. Cycles of American settlement, Native defense of their land, and U.S. military retaliation against the Tetons continued. The army attacked other American Indian peoples as well. In some cases, the Tetons helped defend other groups. For example, Oglala warriors under the leadership of the renowned Crazy Horse (1842–1877) came to the aid of the Cheyennes when they were attacked by the U.S. Army in 1876.

Some Americans living in eastern cities began to oppose the increasing conflict in the plains. They were disturbed by their own government's policies toward American Indians and were shocked by the deaths of thousands of innocent people in Native communities. Leaders of the Tetons and other plains peoples were sometimes invited to speak to various organizations concerned with the plight of Natives. For instance, the Teton leader Red Cloud traveled to New York City in 1871 to address members of the Cooper Institute. Red Cloud's impassioned speech stirred his audience to urge their government to bring about peace and justice for the Tetons. Although the sentiments of some Americans were thus moved to support Native peoples, their ideals did little to influence government policies. (For additional information on this Teton chief, enter "Chief Red Cloud" into any search engine and browse the many sites listed.)

Indeed, in March 1876, the U.S. government responded to the crisis created by intrusions of settlers into the plains by ordering the cavalry to round up all of the Lakotas and force them to remain on their reservations. More pressure was put on the Tetons to give up the sacred Black Hills. The commissioner of Indian affairs, Edward Smith, urged the Tetons to sell the Black Hills "for the sake of promoting the mining and agricultural interests of white men." Commissioner Smith's statement clearly violated his supposed role as protector of American Indians' rights. Then, in 1877, following the Tetons' continued refusal to sell, the U.S. Congress chose to ignore the terms of the Treaty of 1868 and passed an act to take the Black Hills from the Tetons. Congress also unilaterally claimed that all "unceded Indian territory" named in the treaty belonged to the U.S. government.

During the same period, some influential politicians and public figures put forth proposals to expel the Lakotas from their reservations in South Dakota and force them to move to "Indian Territory" in present-day Oklahoma. Although these suggestions were never put into operation, they revealed the attitude of many public officials concerning the government's power to ignore the wishes and rights of American Indians.

And still the crisis continued. Indeed, it worsened. The U.S. Army and militias made up of American vigilantes attacked many Native villages, killing the inhabitants and plundering their property. Soldiers and members of private militias were allowed to keep whatever goods they took from American Indians. One of the many accounts recalling the period had been given by the Oglala spiritual leader Black Elk.

Black Elk described a raid commanded by Colonel J. J. Reynolds against an Oglala village led by Crazy Horse. The raid occurred on March 16, 1876:

> Crazy Horse stayed with about a hundred tepees on the Powder River. It was just daybreak. There was a blizzard and it was very cold. The people were sleeping. Suddenly there were many shots and horses galloping through the village. It was the cavalry of the Wasichus [Americans], and they were yelling and shooting and riding their horses against the tepees. All the people rushed out and ran, because they were not awake yet and they were frightened. The soldiers killed as many women and children and men as they could while the people were running toward a bluff. Then they set fire to some of the tepees and knocked the others down. But when the people were on the side of the bluff, Crazy Horse said something, and all the warriors began singing the death song and charged back upon the soldiers; and the soldiers ran, driving many of the people's ponies ahead of them. Crazy Horse followed them all that day with a band of warriors, and that night he took all the stolen ponies away from them, and brought them back to the village.

The soldiers continued to come. In June 1876, Oglala warriors defended their communities against renewed attacks by the U.S. Army. They stopped a cavalry unit in Montana that was headed for Teton territory. In response, the United States sent a large expedition of six hundred soldiers against the Tetons. The army unit was led by Lieutenant Colonel George Custer. Custer and his soldiers attacked a settlement of Teton people who were camped along the Little Bighorn River in southern Montana. Among the Tetons was Sitting Bull (1834–1890), the famed leader of the Hunkpapa Tetons. During the ensuing battle between the Tetons and Custer's soldiers, Teton warriors from other communities and warriors from other groups such as the Cheyenne came to defend Native land and lives. In the end, the American Indians were victorious. They killed Custer's entire unit, including Custer.

But the victory of the Tetons and their allies did not stop the U.S. Army from continuing its attacks against American Indians. Seeking refuge and respite from the turmoil, Sitting Bull led his group into Canada. They hoped conditions would improve and they would be able to return in peace. Unfortunately, Sitting Bull returned to South Dakota in 1881 and surrendered to the U.S. government at Fort Buford, Montana, on July 19. He hoped, as others had before him, that peace would be established. But the tranquility he desired was not to be found.

After suffering numerous attacks, other Teton chiefs decided to surrender to the U.S. government. They hoped that if they surrendered and renounced warfare, their people would be protected from further conflicts. In 1877, Crazy Horse had agreed to go to Fort Robinson, Nebraska, to negotiate peace with U.S. officials. As soon as he arrived at the fort, however, he was arrested and imprisoned. Black Elk recounted the events of September 5, 1877:

> They told Crazy Horse they would not harm him if he would go and have a talk with the Wasichu chief there. But they lied. They did not take him to the chief for a talk. They took him to the little prison with iron bars on the windows, for they had planned to get rid of him. And when he saw what they were doing, he turned around and took a knife out of his robe and started out against all those soldiers. A soldier ran a bayonet into Crazy Horse from one side and he fell down and began to die.
>
> Crazy Horse was dead. He was brave and good and wise. He never wanted anything but to save his people, and he fought the Wasichus only when they came to kill us in our own country. He was only thirty years old. They could not kill him in battle. They had to lie to him and kill him that way.

During the same period in which warfare was intensifying in the plains, another disastrous event was unfolding. In keeping with the U.S. government's aim of forcing American Indians to change their way of life, officials ordered soldiers to slaughter the herds of buffalo that still roamed the plains. In addition, they encouraged American and European sportsmen and hunters to take part in destroying the buffalo. Without buffalo to supply food, the American Indians would be starved into submitting to terms of treaties favored by the government. The government also hoped that if the buffalo were eliminated, the Tetons and other American Indians would have to give up their hunting and nomadic traditions and become farmers.

Efforts to kill the buffalo intensified during the 1860s and 1870s. Many uses were found for products made from buffalo. During the American Civil War (1861–1865), the U.S. Army had used buffalo hides to make clothing and leather boots and belts for the soldiers. Then, during the 1870s, markets for buffalo hides expanded in Europe as well. Coats and hats made of buffalo hide became very popular in European cities. Leather from buffalo skins was used to make belts, boots, and other articles of clothing. It was also used to manufacture various household utensils and equipment.

Demand for other products made from buffalo increased at the same time. European manufacturers of bone china sought buffalo skeletons to make into powder for use in the production of china dishes. Enormous numbers of bones were used in this process. One of the many companies that bought buffalo bones to sell to manufacturers of china estimated that in the seven years between 1884 and 1891, it obtained bones from 5.95 million buffalo skeletons.

The demand for buffalo products on the part of commercial interests occurred together with the U.S. government's policy of eliminating buffalo as a source of food for American Indians. The result was the slaughter of millions of buffalo and the destruction of the Native peoples' way of life.

U.S. officials voiced strong support for this slaughter. For example, in 1867, Colonel R.I. Dodge, who was in charge of Nebraska's Fort McPherson, told a visiting British hunter named Sir W.F. Butler, "Kill every buffalo you can. Every buffalo dead is an Indian gone."

Similar sentiments were expressed by General Phil Sheridan in 1870, when he encouraged the state legislature in Texas to issue bronze medals of honor to American buffalo hunters. Sheridan suggested that the medals be designed with a drawing on each side: "a dead buffalo on one side and a discouraged Indian on the other."

The scene on the plains was one of death. Many descriptions of this period have been recorded by historians. One account, by Stanley Vestal, noted that "in a brief two years [1873–1875], where there had been myriads of buffalo, there were only myriads of rotting carcasses. The air was filled with the sickening stench of death."

After the surrender of Sitting Bull in 1881, Teton men and women realized their freedom was limited and their way of life had changed. They decided to remain on the lands reserved for them in treaties with the United States. The Tetons hoped that they would finally be left in peace and security. But critical events further interfered with their hopes.

In the 1880s, the U.S. government embarked on a decisive new policy regarding American Indians. The policy was put forth in 1887 in a piece of legislation passed by Congress that was called the General Allotment Act, also known as the *Dawes Act*. The Dawes Act spelled out methods for dividing land in American Indian reservations into small allotments that would be assigned to individual families. It stipulated that American Indian reservations should be divided into allotments of 160 acres. Every family could apply for an allotment and be assigned a specific place to live. The act also stated that any land remaining on reservations after every Native family received its share would be open for sale to American settlers.

Sitting Bull (1834–1890), or Tatanka Iyotanka, was a Hunkpapa Teton chief and holy man who helped lead a combined force of Arapahos, Cheyennes, and Lakotas in their overwhelming victory over U.S. troops at the Battle of the Little Bighorn on June 25, 1876.

The Dawes policy undermined traditional Native values concerning land ownership. According to the customs of most Native Americans, the land under control of a tribe was available to all members who needed it. The land belonged to the whole group, not to specific individuals. But U.S. officials wanted American Indians to divide their land into small plots. They thought that individual ownership of land would encourage American Indians to take up farming. Officials also were opposed to the Native custom of living in large households composed of extended families. They wanted American Indians to live in small households made up of a husband and wife and their children. They hoped this pattern would foster American values.

All of the government's programs showed a bias against ways of life developed by American Indians throughout the centuries. The government ignored American Indians' wishes to be in control of their own lives and to follow their valued traditions.

The Tetons and most other plains peoples were opposed to accepting the allotments. They resisted applying for allotments, preferring instead to maintain their traditional families and living patterns. Still, the government continued to pressure American Indians to comply with the Dawes Act. As an inducement, *agents* in charge of distributing treaty annuities and rations gave these items only to those Teton people who agreed to become farmers. Any people who did not farm were often denied their rightful share.

After 1889, pressure on the Teton people increased. In November of that year, South Dakota was granted statehood. Since most of the state's territory was actually composed of the Great Sioux Reservation as defined in the Treaty of 1868, Americans living in South Dakota urged the federal government to force the Tetons to accept allotments and open the remaining land for sale. In this way, settlers hoped to decrease the size of the reservation and to claim land for themselves. And, as had always happened in the past, the federal government chose to aid American settlers rather than defend the Tetons against intruders.

In compliance with U.S. interests, the Great Sioux Reservation was broken up into five separate reservations in

1889. They were named Pine Ridge, Rosebud, Standing Rock, Cheyenne River, and Lower Brulé. The seven Teton bands were assigned to specific reservations. The Oglalas were to reside on the Pine Ridge Reservation; the Brulés at Rosebud; the Hunkpapas at Standing Rock; both the Miniconjous and the Itazipcos at Cheyenne River; the Sihasapas at either Cheyenne River or Standing Rock; and the Oohenonpas at Cheyenne River and Rosebud.

Land on Teton reservations was allotted to separate families and individuals. By special terms of the Sioux Act, passed by Congress in 1889 to encourage the Tetons to accept allotments, the usual allotment of 160 acres for each family was doubled so that every Teton head of household was assigned a total of 320 acres. Single individuals without families were given 80 acres of land. The remaining territory was open to claims from American settlers. After the policy of allotting land went into effect on February 10, 1890, the reservations carved from the Great Sioux Reservation together comprised approximately half of the Teton's original territory. The other half was sold to American settlers. Once again, terms of the Treaty of 1868 were directly violated by the U.S. government.

The government further negated the treaty by threatening to cut off supplies of rations to the Tetons when they continued to resist accepting allotments. Indeed, officials reduced by half the amount of rations given in the late 1880s and early 1890s. Many Tetons lived on the brink of starvation and many died, owing both to lack of food and to general debilitation and malnutrition. Adding to the calamity, a severe drought occurred during the same period, resulting in the loss of crops grown by some Teton families.

Still, government officials were not content with merely changing the economy of the Tetons; they also wanted to change the Tetons' religious and cultural traditions. The BIA then designed programs that were aimed at managing the lives of American Indians. Although the bureau was established in part to protect American Indians' rights, its officials often acted to undermine Natives' freedom. During the 1870s, the bureau was headed by Thomas Morgan, commissioner of Indian affairs, who directed programs aimed at eradicating American Indians' traditional ways of life. The Tetons, as well as other Natives throughout the United States, were affected by Morgan's plans.

Teton religion and family life came under attack. Protestant and Catholic clergymen were sent to convert the Tetons to Christianity. These missionaries preached against Teton beliefs and tried to persuade the people to give up their traditional ceremonies.

The government also sent teachers to set up boarding schools on the reservations. Teton children were forcibly separated from their families and housed in dormitories at these boarding schools. The children were not allowed to speak the Lakota language. Teachers wanted to isolate children from their parents and communities so that they could be more easily indoctrinated into accepting American values. Even during the summer, when schools were not in session, children were not permitted to return to their families. Instead, they were sent to work as domestic servants in the house-holds of American settlers and government employees.

By 1890, the combination of many different government policies had a devastating effect on the Tetons. Most of the territory on which they had once lived had been taken from them, the buffalo they had hunted were mostly gone, and their beliefs and ways of living were under constant attack. The people wondered if they would ever again be able to establish a good life for themselves.

5

A Dream Denied

For many Tetons, hope for peace and prosperity were answered for a time in the promise of a new religion that was spreading among American Indians throughout western North America. The new religion was popularized by a Paiute man named Wovoka (c. 1860–1932) who lived in Nevada. It has become known as the *Ghost Dance religion*. Wovoka (also known by his English name, Jack Wilson) began to promote the religion in 1889 after having a dramatic visionary experience during a total eclipse of the sun on January 1 of that year. In his vision, Wovoka was taken to heaven, where he saw God. God told him to return to Earth and preach a message of peace and friendship. Wovoka urged American Indians to emphasize their traditional ways of relating to each other and to the world around them. He urged them to help one another, to be kind and generous to all. Wovoka said, "You must not fight. Do no harm to anyone. Do always right."

The Tetons first heard of the new religion in 1889. They were told of it by more westerly groups such as the Arapahos and Shoshones. A delegation of Teton leaders traveled to Nevada late in 1889 to hear the message directly from Wovoka himself. The delegation included Good Thunder from the Pine Ridge Reservation, Short Bull from the Rosebud Reservation, and Kicking Bear from the Cheyenne River Reservation. In April of the following year, these men reported that they had met with Wovoka and that his words were good and true. The religion began to spread rapidly through all the Teton communities. People eagerly sought a faith that gave them hope for a renewed life of harmony and well-being.

In addition to the moral principles that Wovoka emphasized, the Ghost Dance religion included a prophesy that the world as it then was would soon come to an end. The earth would tremble mightily, and after the cataclysm, only the American Indians would remain in North America. Everyone else would disappear. The prophesy also predicted that all the American Indians who had died would return and rejoin their families and friends. The buffalo would return to roam the plains and prairies in great numbers as they had done in earlier times. The life that Native people had once known before the arrival of Europeans would be restored.

In order to prepare for this event, believers of the new religion conducted ceremonies and dances of celebration and hope. Each tribe performed the rites in its own way, often adding to or elaborating on specific themes and performing its special songs and dances.

Many Teton rites began with the following song, expressing belief in the return of the dead:

> The father says so.
> The father says so.
> You shall see your grandfather.
> The father says so.
> You shall see your kindred.
> The father says so.

During the late 1880s, the Ghost Dance religion, which promoted a return to traditional Indian ways and a reunion with the dead, spread through the West. One of its devotees was Kicking Bear (seen here) who helped introduce the religion to the Tetons.

Individuals often composed their own songs, some of which became widely popular among all Teton worshipers. The following song was composed by a young woman who encountered a vision of her deceased mother:

> Mother, come home; mother, come home.
> My little brother goes about always crying,
> My little brother goes about always crying.
> Mother, come home; mother, come home.

Another Teton song expressed themes of renewal and restoration of past ways of living:

> The whole world is coming,
> A nation is coming, a nation is coming.
> The Eagle has brought the message to the tribe.
> The father says so, the father says so.
> Over the whole earth, they are coming.
> The buffalo are coming, the buffalo are coming.
> The Crow has brought the message to the tribe.
> The father says so, the father says so.

Rituals of the Ghost Dance religion included prayers and offerings to spirits as well as songs and dances celebrating the return of the dead and restoration of a renewed way of life. Descriptions of ceremonies were occasionally made by Americans who had contact with Teton believers. J.F. Asay, an American trader living at the Pine Ridge agency, described one ritual that took place in 1890:

> The dancers first stood in line facing the sun, while the leader, standing facing them, made a prayer and waved over their heads the "ghost stick," a staff about six feet long, trimmed with red cloth and feathers of the same color. After thus waving the stick over them, he faced the sun and made another prayer, after which the line closed up to form a circle around the tree [which had been placed in the dance

ground] and the dance began. During the prayer a woman standing near the tree held out a pipe toward the sun, while another beside her held out four arrows from which the points had been removed.

Participants then proceeded to sing and dance. As they did so, they often saw visions of their deceased relatives and received messages from the spirit world.

Not surprisingly, the message of return and renewal had great appeal to people who had been devastated by warfare, poverty, starvation, and disease. They listened to the words of hope spoken to them and participated in dances and songs dedicated to achieving the dream of peace and prosperity.

And, not surprisingly, the U.S. government and settlers were alarmed by the prophesy predicting their disappearance. But American farmers and ranchers invented and exaggerated the danger posed to them by adherents of the Ghost Dance religion. They imagined that American Indians would descend upon their communities, hastening their demise. Such attacks were in no way a part of the religion. Ghost Dance participants never organized raids against settlers. But settlers' fears were aroused and used to enflame hostility against the Tetons and other Native peoples.

Government officials often added to the already tense situation by advocating military action against believers in the Ghost Dance religion. For instance, a man named Daniel F. Royer, who headed the BIA's agency at the Pine Ridge Reservation, wrote to his superiors in Washington, D.C., on October 30, 1890:

> Your Department has been informed of the damage resulting from these dances and of the danger attending them of the crazy Indians doing serious damage to others. I have carefully studied the matter and have brought all the persuasion to bear on the leaders that was possible but without effect and

the only remedy for this matter is the use of military and until this is done you need not expect any progress from these people on the other hand you will be made to realize that they are tearing down more in a day than the Government can build in a month.

Another federal agent, James McLaughlin, in charge of the BIA's office on the Standing Rock Reservation, told Sitting Bull that the Ghost Dance religion was "absurd." He said that Sitting Bull should stop the people at Standing Rock from participating in the dances. Sitting Bull responded by suggesting that both he and McLaughlin travel to Nevada to hear Wovoka's message directly from the spiritual leader himself. Sitting Bull said that if the doctrine was false, he would do whatever he could to persuade his people to ignore it. McLaughlin refused. Instead, on November 19, 1890, he asked officials of the BIA to allow him to withhold rations from people remaining in Sitting Bull's village at Standing Rock. Only those people who moved to the agency's grounds would be given food to eat. Most people did not comply even under the threat of starvation in the bitter winter that was already under way.

In response to growing fears on the part of Americans living in former Teton territory, the government outlawed the Tetons' participation in Ghost Dances. From time to time, soldiers were sent to break up dances and arrest those people deemed responsible for leading them. In November 1890, President Benjamin Harrison gave Secretary of War Redfield Proctor instructions to "suppress any threatened outbreak" of the Ghost Dance.

This order was immediately put into effect. On November 20, 1890, more than one thousand U.S. troops entered the Pine Ridge and Rosebud Reservations. They set up guards around agency offices and government installations, including the Oglala boarding school at Pine Ridge. Children in the school, numbering one hundred, were not permitted to leave nor were their parents allowed to enter.

Tensions at Pine Ridge, Standing Rock, and surrounding communities increased during the next few weeks. Then, on December 15, McLaughlin ordered the arrest of Sitting Bull. Police came at dawn to Sitting Bull's cabin at Standing Rock and tried to arrest him. His supporters were also present. Shots rang out from both sides. Sitting Bull was killed by one of the policemen. Others, both Tetons and Americans, also were shot and killed.

General Nelson Miles, commander of the army in Lakota territory, soon ordered troops to arrest another Teton leader named Big Foot. Big Foot was a chief of the Miniconjou band of Teton. He was well known as a peaceful man and as a negotiator between the Tetons and U.S. officials, but he, too, became a victim in the developing storm stirred by fears and exaggerations. When Big Foot was invited by other Teton leaders to come to the agency at Pine Ridge in order to help negotiate a peaceful resolution of the crisis, he was intercepted by the Seventh Cavalry under the command of Major Samuel Whitside at Fort Bennet. Big Foot was ordered to go to Fort Bennet but he decided instead to continue his trip to Pine Ridge to negotiate peace.

Big Foot and his followers set up camp at Wounded Knee Creek on December 28, 1890. The group consisted of approximately 120 men and 230 women and children. They were immediately surrounded by the U.S. Army. The next day, December 29, Big Foot and his people were told to give up all of their guns. Most did so, but some still held on to their weapons. The confrontation became more intense. Shots rang out from the soldiers and from the Tetons defending themselves. The army responded by massacring the people. More than three hundred were killed, later to be buried in a mass grave. Two-thirds of the victims were women and children. Big Foot also died in the attack. One eyewitness to the tragedy, a Teton man named Turning Hawk, later described the scene:

> All the men who were in a bunch were killed right there, and
> those who escaped that first fire got into the ravine, and as

Big Foot, a chief of the Miniconjou band of Teton, was one of more than three hundred Native Americans (two-thirds of whom were women and children) who were killed by the U.S. Army at Wounded Knee, South Dakota, on December 29, 1890.

they went along up the ravine for a long distance they were pursued on both sides by the soldiers and shot down, as the dead bodies showed afterwards. The women were standing off at a different place from where the men were stationed, and when the firing began, those of the men who escaped the first onslaught went in one direction up the ravine, and then the women, who were bunched together at another place, went entirely in a different direction through an open field, and the women fared the same fate as the men who went up the deep ravine.

Another witness, American Horse, added more details: "The women as they were fleeing with their babies were killed together, shot right through, and the women who were very heavy with child were also killed. All the Indians fled, and after most all of them had been killed a cry was made that those who were not killed or wounded should come forth and they would be safe. Little boys who were not wounded came out of their places of refuge, and as soon as they came in sight a number of soldiers surrounded them and butchered them there."

When other Tetons residing at Pine Ridge heard news of the massacre, they fled the area for fear that they, too, would be killed. Soon thereafter, most of the Tetons returned and their leaders surrendered to government authorities. The last Teton chief to surrender was Kicking Bear. He finally gave in to the United States on January 15, 1891.

The tragic events that occurred at Wounded Knee aroused enough outrage on the part of some influential Americans to call for an official investigation into the massacre. As a result of these demands, the public heard for the first time about the deplorable living conditions of the Teton people. Inquiries were held in 1891 to hear testimony and receive reports from government officials, missionaries, and army officers who described life for the Tetons. In one account, General Nelson Miles noted that the Lakotas had "signed away a valuable portion of their reservation, and it is now occupied by white people, for which they [the Lakotas] have received nothing. They understood that ample provision would be made for their support; instead, their supplies have been reduced and much of the time they have been living on half and two-thirds rations. The disaffection is widespread. These facts are beyond question, and the evidence is positive and sustained by thousands of witnesses."

Miles quoted from a report written by the commander of Fort Yates in North Dakota concerning the Tetons living at Standing Rock. The report listed numerous failures of the U.S. government contributing to the poverty and demoralization of the people. Among them:

- Failure of the government to provide the full allowance of seeds and agricultural implements to Indians engaged in farming.

- Failure of the government to issue such Indians the full number of cows and oxen.

- Failure of the government to issue to the Indians the full amount of *annuity* supplies to which they are entitled.

- Failure of the government to have the clothing and other annuity supplies ready for issue.

- Failure of the government to appropriate money for the payment of the Indians for the ponies taken from them.

The commander concluded that: "It appears that the government has failed to fulfill its obligations, and in order to render the Indians law-abiding, peaceful, contented, and prosperous it is strongly recommended that the treaties be promptly and fully carried out, and that the promises made be faithfully kept."

In another report, Captain J.H. Hurst, commander of Fort Bennet in South Dakota, detailed numerous complaints voiced by the Tetons. They included:

(1) That the boundaries of the reservation are not what they agreed to;

(2) That they have never received full recompense for the
    ponies taken from them;

(3) That the game has been destroyed and driven out of the
    country by the white people;

(4) That their children are taken from them and kept for
    years [at boarding schools] instead of being educated
    among them;

(5) That the rations issued to them are insufficient in quan-
    tity and frequently very poor in quality.

Finally, Bishop W.H. Hare, an Episcopal minister living at
Pine Ridge, said that starvation, lack of annuity supplies, and
rampant epidemics of measles, whooping cough, and influenza
had decimated the population at Pine Ridge and the other
Teton reservations.

In the context of life as described in written and oral testimony, many Tetons had responded by seeking relief in the hope
given by the Ghost Dance religion's message of spiritual power,
moral renewal, and the future restoration of an earlier way of
living. The U.S. government, however, reacted by subjecting the
Tetons to further deprivation, and the army responded with
increased military force.

The massacre of innocent people at Wounded Knee Creek
on December 29, 1890, has come to be a symbol of the plight
of Native people throughout North America. The people's
hope for a new life and their dream of harmony and justice
were answered with brutal death and burial in a mass grave.

But still the Tetons survived. Their will to endure remained
strong as they faced new challenges, accepting changes in their
lives but maintaining their determination to hold on to their
own cultural traditions.

6

Seeking a New Way

In the early years of the twentieth century, the Tetons began a slow process of adopting a new lifestyle. Their faith in their own traditions remained strong but they also realized that the old ways were gone forever. Economic and political changes were forced upon them by the U.S. government and its agencies. In this context, the people sought to establish a life for themselves that incorporated necessary changes but remained true to their own values.

At the turn of the twentieth century, even after many years of government pressure, most Tetons had not accepted individual allotments. They preferred to hold their land communally. But within a few decades, the BIA succeeded in dividing all of the Teton reservations into allotted shares. The policy proved to be disastrous for several reasons. First, after allotments were assigned to each family, the remaining land was declared "surplus" and was sold either to the U.S. government or to American farmers and ranchers. This process resulted in a loss of millions of acres for the Tetons.

Second, more land was lost when individual owners were permitted to sell their land. According to procedures outlined by the Dawes Act of 1887, allotted land was held in trust for a period of twenty-five years. An owner could not sell his or her land during that time but could do so after the trust period ended. Many Teton people did agree to sell their land, some out of ignorance or from trickery and some because of dire poverty and the need to obtain money to support themselves.

A final unfortunate result of allotment policies stemmed from procedures concerning the inheritance of land. Since ownership passes to all descendants, some pieces of land are now owned by more than one hundred people. Decisions about how to use the land often involve many owners and become so complicated that nothing actually gets done.

All of the Teton reservations have suffered from the various effects of allotment policies. Loss of land is the most significant problem, because without land, the people lose any possibility of economic development and prosperity. For example, by 1934, the Rosebud Reservation had lost 2,195,905 acres of its original territory. Most of this land was sold to outsiders, although some was ceded to the U.S. government. A second example concerns the Pine Ridge Reservation, which originally contained 2,721,597 acres of land. During the years between 1904 and 1916, a total of 8,275 individual plots, amounting to 2,380,195 acres, were assigned to Teton landowners. The "surplus" land of 182,653 acres was sold to the U.S. government. Only about 147,000 acres remained under tribal ownership. Since then, more than half of the land given out in allotments has passed out of Native control. Some has been sold and the rest leased to outside farmers and ranchers. The Tetons, therefore, currently control less than half of their original reservation territory.

A sign marks the entrance to Pine Ridge Reservation, near the border of South Dakota and Nebraska. One of five reservations to be partitioned from the Great Sioux Reservation in 1889, Pine Ridge is currently the largest Lakota reservation with 15,507 residents.

Still, despite these serious problems, many Teton people were able to prosper. By the time of World War I, the Oglalas at Pine Ridge had successfully developed large herds of cattle. They also raised many horses, and became the breeders of some of the best horses in North America. Since these enterprises were communally controlled, all of the people benefited. Then, in 1917, after the United States entered World War I, the BIA agent in charge of Pine Ridge sold all of the Oglalas' cattle on the pretext that they were needed for the war effort. Rangeland on which the Oglalas' cattle had formerly grazed was then leased to non-Indian cattle herders.

After the war ended, more land was leased to outsiders. Large agricultural companies were expanding their acreage and succeeded in persuading the BIA to allow the leasing of land on Teton reservations to their enterprises.

And so the Tetons continued to lose access to their own land. As a result, the population on the reservations gradually became split into two groups. One group retained control of their land and continued to make a living from farming and ranching. The other group consisted of landless people who migrated to agency towns on the reservations. There, they sought work to support themselves. But since the only work available in towns was connected to the federal government, these people became dependent on the BIA agent and other officials for their jobs.

Federal policy toward American Indians began to change in the 1930s under the New Deal policies promoted by President Franklin D. Roosevelt. At that time, the commissioner of Indian affairs, John Collier, developed a new program aimed at changing the relations between American Indians and the federal government. Collier's policies were, in part, a response to a national report on living conditions on reservations through-out the United States. The report, called the Meriam Report, after its principal writer, Lewis M. Meriam, was issued in 1928 after several years of intensive research. The Meriam Report reviewed living conditions, health status, educational programs and achievements, and governing structures on American Indian reservations. After examining the evidence, the report vigorously condemned the Dawes Act of 1887 and the ensuing policies of the federal government. It condemned the breakup of American Indians' territory and the shrinkage of their land base. It noted the deplorable living conditions and health status endured by Native peoples, and it criticized the educational system that forced American Indian children to leave their families and communities to be taught in boarding schools.

The Meriam Report made significant recommendations to reorient federal policy. It urged ending the boarding school system and replacing it with an extensive network of day schools on reservations. It also urged that tribal groups themselves have more power to make decisions concerning programs and policies affecting their communities. In addition, the Meriam Report stressed the right of American Indians to maintain their language and cultural traditions if they chose to do so.

Influenced by the findings and recommendations of the Meriam Report, John Collier's efforts to revamp government policy culminated in Congress' passage of the *Indian Reorganization Act* (IRA) of 1934. The act principally provided for establishment of limited self-government on reservations. Each reservation was able to adopt a tribal constitution and set up a tribal council based on elections by members of the tribe. These councils were given responsibility to manage federal and local programs operating on their reservations. They were given authority to develop economic resources as tribal enterprises, and they had the task of helping to manage and carry out efforts toward improving living standards, health, and education for their people.

Collier was also able to convince Congress to appropriate funds for two special projects. A total of $2 million per year was to be spent to purchase new land adjacent to reservations in order to restore at least some of the territory lost through earlier treaty violations. And $5 million per year was granted for programs of economic development and educational improvement on reservations.

In accordance with the IRA's provisions, the Teton reservations adopted tribal constitutions and established councils in 1935. This shift to self-government has been beneficial in its emphasis on local control and local decision-making. However, previous problems that stemmed from loss of access to land have continued and, indeed, increased. Many landless people have now become dependent for their jobs on patronage from members of tribal councils. Political control by a few over many has therefore only shifted from BIA agents to local tribal councils.

Divisions between rural dwellers and townspeople have grown sharper. These splits not only reflect a difference in preference of residence but also involve differences in attitudes toward Teton life. Rural residents tend to retain their use of the Lakota language and to be involved in traditional religious, social, and cultural events. In contrast, townspeople tend to speak English and adopt other facets of American culture.

Despite these significant differences, though, all Tetons are faced with many of the same problems. As a tribe, issues concerning land and its use have remained paramount. Their territory, although guaranteed by treaties, continues to be in jeopardy. For example, when the federal government built an extensive system of dams along the Missouri River in the late 1940s and early 1950s, land on two Teton reservations was flooded in the process. The Standing Rock Reservation and the Cheyenne River Reservation lost most of their arable and wooded land. One dam in particular, the Oahe Dam, flooded 160,889 acres of the best rangeland and farms on the reservations. Nearly all timber resources and wild fruit areas were also destroyed.

The need to develop tribal economies and to provide jobs for residents continues to be a major concern for the Tetons. Federal policies have sometimes undermined their efforts to establish thriving enterprises on the reservations. Sale of their successful cattle herds during World War I and destruction of their most valuable farmland and timber resources in the building of dams took away much of the income generated by the Tetons. As a result, levels of unemployment were extremely high, reaching as much as seventy percent. Without independent economic ventures to produce jobs, half of those people who work on the reservations are employed by federal or local government organizations.

As a response to widespread poverty on American Indian reservations throughout the country, the BIA instituted a new policy in the 1950s aimed at encouraging American Indians to leave their reservations and move to cities where jobs were supposedly available. Through the so-called relocation program, the government provided funds to pay for transportation to a city and, in some cases, to help pay the fees for job training. Although some Tetons agreed to relocate to such cities as Rapid City, South Dakota; Minneapolis, Minnesota; Green Bay, Wisconsin; and Denver, Colorado, most chose to remain in their home communities where they continued to have the social support of their families and friends. And for those people who did relocate, many returned when they found that few jobs were actually available for them. Without jobs, city-dwellers often ended up living in poor urban ghettos.

During the 1960s, programs related to President Lyndon Johnson's "War on Poverty" provided an influx of jobs on Teton reservations. However, access to these jobs was often dependent on the old system of patronage, through which positions were given out by members of tribal councils. The power of councilors thus increased during this period.

The Tetons were affected by other trends that were occurring during the 1960s as well. Many American Indians throughout North America became involved in political organizations aimed at strengthening Native rights and safeguarding provisions guaranteed in treaties. Issues of maintaining and restoring land originally within reservation boundaries and of hunting and fishing rights were especially important. Many Tetons and other Lakotas became very active in promoting goals of Native organizations. Some took part in efforts to bring local and national attention to the needs of American Indians. For example, in 1964, after the federal government closed a prison on Alcatraz Island in San Francisco Bay and declared the land "excess property," a number of Lakotas living in San Francisco filed a suit in court to claim the island. Although their suit was dismissed, the action brought attention to questions of land ownership and control that are vitally important to Native peoples.

The claim of the Lakotas in San Francisco laid the ground-work for a major action in November 1969, when more than a hundred American Indians from all over the United States took over the prison grounds on Alcatraz Island. Since the San Francisco American Indian Center had recently burned down, the people asked that the island be used as a site for a new American Indian community center. The group of activists formed an organization called Indians of All Tribes, stressing the mutual problems facing all Native peoples. They remained on the island for nineteen months. In the end, they were evicted by U.S. marshals. However, during the occupation, the group was able to bring national attention to the conditions and concerns of American Indians.

In addition to participating in many Native organizations and activities, several Teton men were among the founders of one of the most militant American Indian rights groups, the *American Indian Movement* (AIM). AIM was established in 1968 among urban American Indians living in Minneapolis, Minnesota. Its founders were Russell Means, Dennis Banks, both Tetons, and two Chippewa brothers, Vernon and Clyde Bellecourt. AIM's goals were similar to those of other Native rights organizations, but their methods were sometimes more confrontational. Members of AIM believed that it was often necessary to publicly confront people who held political power, both on reservations and in the state and federal systems. They organized demonstrations to arouse the public, both locally and nationally, concerning conditions faced by American Indians in the United States. Issues related to legal rights, treaty obligations, and land losses were of major concern. (For additional information on this organization, enter "American Indian Movement (AIM)" into any search engine and browse the many sites listed.)

AIM members took part in a national demonstration in 1972 called the Trail of Broken Treaties. This effort was planned to focus attention on the long history of the government's failure to keep promises it made in treaties with American Indians. Loss of land, violation of treaty obligations, and denial

Russell Means (left) and Dennis Banks (right) helped found the American Indian Movement (AIM) in 1968. The organization's purpose is to encourage self-determination among Native Americans and to establish international recognition of their treaty rights.

of Native rights were all issues brought before the public as American Indian marchers walked from Seattle to Washington, D.C. They ended their march at the offices of the BIA in the nation's capital. There they barricaded themselves in the bureau's building and pledged to remain until their demands were addressed. They stayed for six days, reviewing files and releasing documents that they said showed the agency's negligence in carrying out its supposed goal of protecting American Indians' rights.

During 1972, several local events occurred that had an immediate impact on people in Teton communities. One was the murder of Raymond Yellow Thunder, an Oglala man from Pine Ridge. He was set upon by two men in Gordon, Nebraska, who stripped him of his clothes and forced him to enter an American Legion hall where a dance was in progress. Then he

A pony mask from the National Museum of the American Indian, Washington, D.C. During dances and parades, warriors wore masks like this one, which celebrated their achievements in battle.

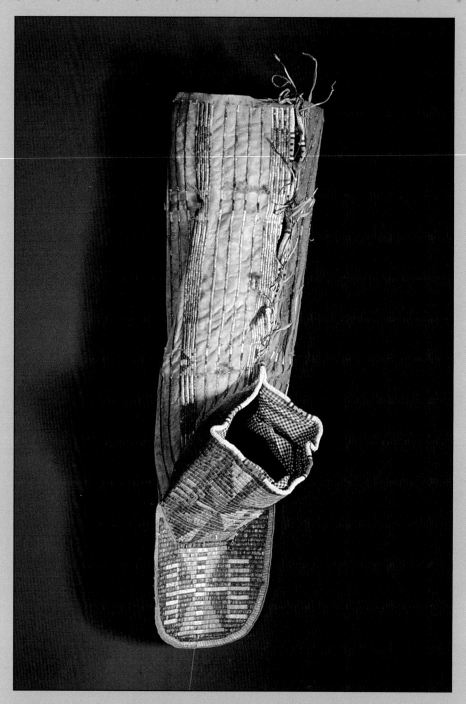

A Lakota baby-carrier with embroidered quillwork from the Staatliche Museum, Berlin, Germany.

Housed at the British Museum in London, this beadwork decoration on a sleeveless jacket shows a confrontation between a Lakota and a white man.

A Lakota cradle most likely made from the hide of a buffalo. The Lakotas used nearly every part of the buffalo to make clothing and implements that were an integral part of their everyday lives.

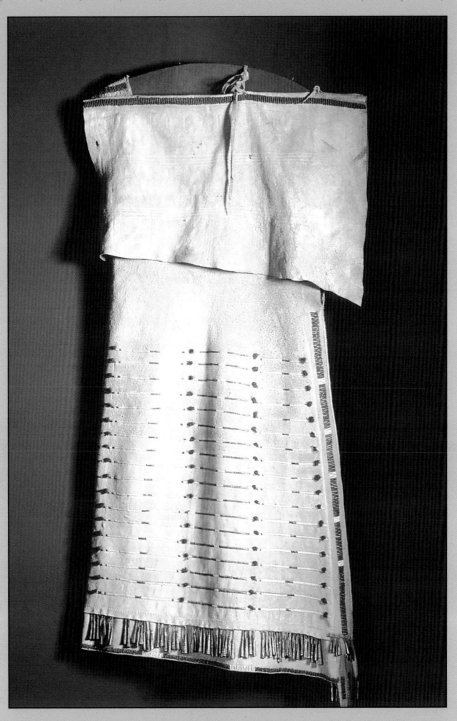

Lakota woman's dress, c. 1830, housed at the Staatliche Museum, Berlin, Germany.

A pair of quilted Lakota moccasins, c. 1895, from the Plains Indian Museum, Cody, Wyoming.

Late nineteenth-century Lakota dress decorated with beadwork.

Lakota warrior's shirt, c. 1849, decorated with quillwork, pigment, and hair.

was beaten so severely that he died of his injuries. Despite the brutality of the attacks, his tormentors and killers were only charged with second-degree manslaughter, rather than murder. They served one year in jail for their crime. People at Pine Ridge and the other Teton reservations, as well as Tetons living in urban areas in South Dakota, were outraged by the murder of Yellow Thunder and by the light punishment meted out to his killers. They organized demonstrations in Nebraska of more than two thousand people to protest the system of justice that treats Native American offenders harshly but treats leniently those who commit crimes against Natives.

A second important event of 1972 was the founding of the Oglala Sioux Civil Rights Organization at Pine Ridge. The founders were disturbed by what they saw as corruption and abuse of power by local tribal leaders. This issue stemmed from the long-standing problem of control over tribal affairs wielded by tribal councilors and the tribal president. In 1972, a bitter election campaign for president of the tribal council took place between Gerald One Feather and Richard Wilson. One Feather represented the more traditional residents of Pine Ridge who were keenly interested in preserving Teton cultural traditions and ways of living. Wilson represented the townspeople who tended to be more oriented toward American values and lifestyles. The contest between One Feather and Wilson symbolized the split in ideology between rural and town dwellers in the Teton population.

Wilson won the election and immediately attempted to block the activities of his opponents. He persuaded the tribal council to ban AIM from the Pine Ridge Reservation. Then he formed an Oglala police force to help enforce the ban. The two primary founders of AIM, Russell Means and Dennis Banks, became particular targets of Wilson's campaign.

As could be expected, Wilson's policies highlighted and intensified divisions among people at Pine Ridge. His supporters said that his actions were necessary to maintain peace on the reservation and to keep "outside agitators" from disrupting the community. Wilson's opponents said that he abused his power in order to punish anyone who disagreed with him. They claimed that the reservation police force acted like a "goon squad," mistreating and physically beating Wilson's opponents.

Then, in February 1973, some of the tribal councilors from Pine Ridge formed a group called the Inter-District Council of the Oglala Sioux Tribe. They opposed Wilson's tactics, stating that he was corrupt and abusive. Three of the councilors filed motions to start proceedings to impeach Wilson. Wilson responded by declaring a state of emergency on the reservation and calling in U.S. marshals to keep the peace.

Later that month, several traditional leaders at Pine Ridge met to discuss the developing crisis. They decided to invite Russell Means and other members of AIM to come to the reservation and help protect their rights. AIM had previously expressed interest not only in safeguarding Native rights guaranteed by treaties with the federal government but in fighting corruption in tribal politics as well. Its willingness to confront local politicians and power brokers brought it to the attention of the people at Pine Ridge who sought to preserve Teton traditions. After the meeting between AIM and the supporters of traditional ways, Dennis Banks recalled that two of the women made desperate pleas for AIM's support. Banks remembered the words of Helen Moves Camp: "She started to cry during her talk to me. She came right up to me, crying, and she was begging for help. She said that if it's the last thing we do, we should fight for Indian people, and fight there."

According to Helen Moves Camp's recollections, the chiefs then suggested that AIM members go to the village of Wounded Knee on the Pine Ridge Reservation and make their protest there. Banks, Means, and the other AIM members agreed and on February 27 proceeded to Wounded Knee, stopping at the site of the mass grave of victims of the Wounded Knee massacre of 1890. One of the protesters, a spiritual leader named Leonard Crow Dog, offered a prayer at the site and said: "Here we come going the other way. It's just like those Indian soldiers in Big Foot's band who were going to Pine Ridge, and now they're coming back. We're those soldiers, we're those Indian people, we're them, we're back, and we can't go any further."

Returning to Wounded Knee in 1973 to bring attention to the problems that Teton people faced made use of the powerful symbol of the oppression of American Indians in North America. The feelings of participants were expressed by Dennis Banks:

> We all knew when he [Leonard Crow Dog] got done talking that we would have to do or die at Wounded Knee. Everything pointed to one course of action—retake Wounded Knee. The medicine men brought wisdom to us. They gave us the spiritual direction we needed. There was no writing letters to the government and sending them demands any more. That's exactly what the medicine men said to us—"when you put your words on paper, then they step on them." So the direction that we received was good.

As news of the occupation of Wounded Knee spread throughout the United States, hundreds of Native and non-Native supporters came to Pine Ridge. Within a few weeks, three hundred American Indians were barricaded in the village, determined to remain until the federal government responded to their demands. They called on the government to investigate activities and policies of the BIA and to adhere to promises made in treaties with American Indians. They also wanted the Oglalas to be free to choose their own form of local government instead of being forced to comply with federal policies.

The protesters were surrounded by a force of three hundred federal marshals, FBI agents, and police officers. From time to time, the confrontation erupted into gunfire. By the end of the seventy-one-day occupation, two American Indians had been killed and two were wounded. One federal marshal was also wounded.

Russell Means, Dennis Banks, and more than thirty other demonstrators were charged with a variety of felonies in connection with the occupation, but they were acquitted because of illegal actions taken by the government in pursuing the case. Such actions included the use of illegal wiretaps, paid witnesses, altered evidence, and the perjuring of prosecution witnesses.

And so the community at Wounded Knee became, for a second time, the symbol of American Indians' hopes for a future free from interference from government authorities. The hope remains.

7

Contemporary Issues

The Tetons today face many of the same problems as they did in past years—indeed in past centuries. They strive to retain their territory, to seek justice for their people, and to maintain a harmonious community life. They seek a balance between the changes experienced by all people in the world today and the values derived from their own traditions.

The Tetons continue to be embroiled in controversies concerning land and legal rights. For more than a century, they have struggled to regain possession of the Black Hills, taken from them by an act of Congress in 1877. The issue remains important to the Tetons because it represents a long history of illegal actions by the government against their people. Also, many Teton consider the Black Hills, which they call *Pahasapa*, to be sacred land, inhabited by powerful spirits.

After congressional hearings were held in 1974 regarding the Tetons' claim for the Black Hills, they were awarded a sum of

$17.5 million as compensation for the land. They were also given $85 million in interest payments. The Department of Justice objected to the settlement and appealed to the Court of Claims, a court established to hear cases involving American Indians' land claims. In 1980, the court awarded the Tetons a total of $105 million. This ruling was upheld by the U.S. Supreme Court.

Despite a favorable monetary settlement, the Tetons have refused to accept payment in exchange for title to the Black Hills. Instead, they want the territory returned to them. Their continued claims to the region are based on both the Treaty of 1868 and the American Indian Religious Freedom Act, which Congress passed in 1978. They have appealed to Senator Daniel Inouye (D-HI), vice chairman of the Senate Committee on Indian Affairs, to settle the case. The matter is still pending. Meanwhile, the money awarded to the Tetons remains in trust in a BIA account, collecting interest. (For additional information on the controversy over this sacred Teton location, enter "Black Hills land claim" into any search engine and browse the many sites listed.)

A second lingering legal controversy concerns the case of Leonard Peltier. Peltier, an Oglala activist who at the time was living at Pine Ridge, was involved in an incident that occurred on the reservation in 1975. The details remain unclear, but an exchange of gunfire took place between several Oglala men and four FBI agents. Two of the agents and one Oglala man were killed. Leonard Peltier and three other Oglalas were arrested and charged with murder. Two of the men were put on trial first and both were acquitted. Peltier decided to seek refuge in Canada rather than stand trial because he believed he would not get a fair hearing. After his extradition from Canada, which was protested by many members of the Canadian parliament, Peltier was tried, convicted, and sentenced to life imprisonment.

Peltier and his lawyers have since appealed the verdict and requested a new trial based on evidence they have uncovered

Leonard Peltier was one of several Oglala men involved in a tragic shoot-out with four FBI agents on June 26, 1975, at Pine Ridge Reservation in South Dakota. The details of the incident remain unclear, but Peltier has been serving two life sentences at Leavenworth Prison in Kansas for the deaths of two of the FBI agents.

that shows the government's illegal activities in investigating and prosecuting the case. Among these are tampering with evidence, suppression of ballistics reports, and coercion of prosecution witnesses. Requests for a new trial have been denied repeatedly by the courts, but appeals continue to be filed. Peltier's requests are supported by letters from many members of Congress, by a number of religious leaders throughout the world, and by Amnesty International, a prominent human rights organization that has declared Peltier a political prisoner of conscience.

Although issues such as the Black Hills land claim and the Peltier case have gained national and even international attention, the Tetons are also faced with problems in their home communities. High rates of unemployment, lack of capital to invest in economic enterprises, and poor health-care services continue to be major problems.

However, the Tetons continue to attempt to find solutions to their difficulties, merging new methods with age-old traditions. Participation in community events that express Teton values of harmony, generosity, and cooperation help sustain the people. One such event is the giveaway. A giveaway is a traditional ceremonial distribution of gifts. In earlier times, it occurred at the end of a one-year period of mourning after a death. A year's mourning, called Keeping of the Soul, is one of the Tetons' Seven Sacred Rites. At giveaways, the relatives of the deceased distributed goods to people in the community. Goods of many types were given, but horses and buffalo robes were especially prized.

Today, giveaways are held to mark many important occasions, including births, marriages, and graduations. People now give quilts, clothing, and household items to their guests.

Although the occasions for giveaways and the items distributed have changed, the underlying values expressed by the event remain the same. Gifts are given in order to establish lasting bonds of friendship and cooperation with others. Individuals give to others as a real and symbolic way of showing that they value sharing and generosity. Through acts of giving, they expand the network of people with whom they exchange mutual support and cooperation.

After gifts are given, speeches are offered by men who are specially selected by the host. Speeches include moral lessons directed at young people; teaching them traditional values of harmony and helpfulness to others. The men's speeches are punctuated and followed by a chorus of approval from women in attendance. Afterward, a traditional feast is shared by all.

Other aspects of Teton ceremonial life continue to be important to many in the various reservation communities. Followers of traditional Teton religion mark many of the ancient sacred rites performed by their ancestors. Sun Dances are held often, especially in rural communities where traditions remain strongest. In addition, many people seek to obtain support and instruction from spirits through individual Vision Quests, and many seek advice and care given by traditional healers when they suffer from illness or other misfortunes.

Another aspect of life that is critical to maintaining Teton traditions is knowledge and use of the Lakota language. The language is spoken by many Tetons on the reservations. People living in rural areas and those involved in traditional lifeways are more likely to speak Lakota fluently. Lakota is used especially in traditional religious and social contexts.

In order to ensure continuation of Lakota, the language is taught to children in schools on the reservations. It is taught at all levels of education, including elementary and high school, as well as at the two Teton community colleges—one on Pine Ridge and the other on the Rosebud Reservation.

Schools serving Teton children and adults also offer Indian Studies programs that are dedicated to preserving Teton history and culture.

The Tetons continue to balance the changes brought about by their circumstances with the valued traditions of their heritage. Problems of finding employment on or near reservations still affect hopes for their prosperity. Economic enterprises have been established by the tribe and by individuals, but they are often in danger of failure because of lack of capital to invest and expand. Although many people do find jobs nearby, rates of unemployment and underemployment remain high. Still, the reservation communities survive and provide social support and nurturance for their members and populations on the reservations continue to grow.

8

Tetons in the Twenty-First Century

The Teton Sioux, or the Lakotas as they now usually call themselves, enter the twenty-first century with plans to revitalize their economies and to strengthen their people and their heritage. Many of the problems still facing the people stem from the difficulties of developing and maintaining prosperity in rural areas of the Northern Plains. Their most pressing concern is the need for economic development. All five reservations are located in rural parts of South Dakota, a state that has economic difficulties of its own.

All the Lakota reservations have high rates of poverty due primarily to the lack of jobs. And the lack of jobs is the result of the scarcity of industry and other large employers in the region. However, despite these major difficulties, the reservation communities are responding by trying to create small businesses and other economic projects that will provide jobs for their people and income for their tribes.

Elsie Meeks, who became the first Native American to serve on the U.S. Commission on Civil Rights when she was appointed to the post by then-Senate Majority Leader Tom Daschle (D-SD) in 1999, has been an advocate for bringing small businesses to Pine Ridge Reservation. Meeks is the founder of the Lakota Fund, which provides loans to the Lakota people of southwestern South Dakota who operate small or start-up businesses.

In 1999, national, and even international, attention was centered on the Lakota reservations, especially the community at Pine Ridge, when then-U.S. President Bill Clinton visited the reservation and proposed his "new markets" initiative. At the time, and continuing today, Shannon County, where Pine Ridge Reservation is located, is the poorest county in the entire United States. Because of the dismal economic situation at Pine Ridge, President Clinton made a stop in the community as part of his tour of economically depressed areas and designated it an "empowerment zone." As a result, Pine Ridge became eligible to receive $20 million in federal funds over a period of ten years. The money is earmarked for use to improve infrastructure such as building and paving roads and upgrading electricity and water systems. These efforts will improve the reservation communities and hopefully attract businesses and employment.

Since the initiative was announced, various projects have been undertaken. For example, the reservations have applied for and received federal aid from the Small Business Administration and other government agencies to help develop marketing programs that will aid local businesses. These businesses have a wide range of sales and service potential. At Pine Ridge Reservation, businesses tied to construction are particularly important because of the lack of adequate housing and the poor condition of many of the houses and roads that already exist. Workers are helping to rebuild the community, supplying much-needed housing, schools, and other public facilities.

Since much of the land on the Teton reservations is used for cattle raising, some of the communities are pursuing the development of businesses that process animal meat and other products. For example, the Lower Brulé Sioux tribe obtained a loan from state agencies in South Dakota, which it is utilizing to study the feasibility of starting a beef-processing plant on its reservation. The U.S. Department of Agriculture is also contributing funds for the project. The tribe already has a large herd of cattle, which is the collective property of the Lower Brulé Sioux. The plan is to coordinate the tribe's efforts to develop the processing plant in conjunction with private ranchers on the reservation.

In addition to the beef-processing enterprise, the tribe is studying the possibility of operating a factory that would process locally grown corn. The corn will be used for two purposes. First, it will be made into ethanol, a grain-based fuel additive. Second, the byproducts from the processing would be used to feed cattle. The Lower Brulé project is therefore designed to locally control and benefit from the entire industry of cattle ranching. Since they already own a large herd of animals, the tribe can integrate all of the processes—from cattle raising to supplying meat. By producing their own cattle feed from local corn, establishing slaughterhouses and meat-processing plants, the Lower Brulé project will reap the profits derived from the sale of meat.

Another innovative economic development project has begun operation on the Rosebud Reservation. The Rosebud Sioux have constructed a large wind turbine, a machine that generates power from wind. The Rosebud turbine is the first to be owned and operated by American Indians in the United States. The power it produces is clean and efficient and utilizes a renewable source of energy. Energy generated by the wind turbine will be sold to a local energy company for the benefit of residents of the reservation as well as those living in nearby communities. In addition, the federal government has contracted to purchase energy produced by the wind turbine for use at the Ellsworth Air Force Base near Rapid City, South Dakota. Power from the Rosebud turbine will also be utilized by a number of regional energy consortiums, including the Nebraska Public Power and the Western Area Power Administration.

The Rosebud project makes use of the enormous renewable energy source of the Great Plains—wind. Indeed, the Great Plains has one of the richest potentials for wind-generated energy in the world. According to energy experts: "The two dozen reservations [in the Great Plains] have a combined wind power potential that exceeds 300 gigawatts, or about half the entire installed electrical generation capacity of the United States."

Wind-generated energy is cost-effective and renewable. It also has the benefit of not producing pollution or destroying the air and ground like other energy sources, such as coal and oil. According to South Dakota Senator Tom Daschle, in a statement read at the dedication of the Rosebud turbine: "The development of renewable energy sources, like wind and ethanol, is essential to help reduce our dependence on foreign sources of oil. Tribal lands contain diverse renewable energy resources and can play an important role in shaping national energy policy."

Pat Spears, president of the Intertribal Council on Utility Policy, a group composed of Northern Plains tribes, commented on the importance of the project to the Rosebud economy: "A tribe is only as sovereign as its economy, finances, and actions permit. One of our tribal goals is energy self-sufficiency. Developing our renewable energy resources will help us achieve that goal."

The tribe at the Cheyenne River Reservation is participating, along with other plains tribes, in building up its herds of buffalo, an animal that the Lakota peoples' ancestors depended upon for their survival. The Cheyenne River Sioux have the largest buffalo herd of any plains reservation. They now own some twenty-four hundred animals, accounting for more than one-fifth of the twelve thousand buffalo currently owned by fifty-two North American Indian tribes.

The buffalo herds are important for two reasons. First, the animals are an important ingredient in the tribes' efforts toward economic development and self-sufficiency. The Cheyenne River Sioux and other plains tribes are hoping to profit from the sale of buffalo meat and other animal products. In addition, the Lakotas understand that the resurgence of the buffalo on the plains is a key to returning to and preserving some of their sacred traditions. According to Oglala historian and lawyer, Vine Deloria, Jr.: "What you're seeing are growing attempts of all kinds by Native Americans to return to a more traditional relationship with nature—a restoration of their cultures. The elders have wanted to do this for a long time. Finally, tribes are in a position where they can devote resources to this effort."

In the words of Harry Charger, a Cheyenne River elder: "Our prophecies are beginning to come true. The buffalo are coming back and with them our strength as a people." Another Sioux spiritual leader, Arvol Looking Horse explained: "We and the buffalo are one."

As part of their effort to increase the buffalo population, the Cheyenne River tribe purchased a twenty-two-thousand-acre cattle ranch to allow buffalo to graze. The tribe now owns and manages the land and the buffalo herd collectively. The project planners hope to market buffalo meat for sale to a variety of consumers, including government school lunch programs, Indian-operated casinos throughout the country, and other retail outlets.

Buffalo ranchers are consulting with experts on marketing and range management at the Oglala Lakota College. They are studying the migratory patterns and social structure of buffalo herds. This effort is geared toward understanding buffalo behavior in order to better manage the herds and raise healthier animals. In addition, the meat produced from grass-fed and free-ranging buffalo is superior to that obtained from feedlots. According to Dr. Kim Winkelman, vice president of Oglala Lakota College: "We combine medicine and oral traditions and think holistically about the buffalo. Through science and understanding of the Lakota perspective on science we are validating our oral traditions. What observers and scientists are now learning is what American Indians have known for centuries."

In addition to economic development projects on each reservation, the Lakota tribes are joining together in communal efforts to retain control of their resources. These efforts are undertaken in conjunction with the people's insistence on their rightful ownership of the Black Hills in western South Dakota, a site sacred to all Lakotas. The tribes have become members of the Black Hills Inter-tribal Advisory Committee. The committee is prepared to function as an advisory board to the National Forest Service and its aim is to protect historic and sacred sites in the Black Hills.

The participation of the Lakota tribes in this initiative underscores the people's commitment to preserve their relationship with the sacred territory of the Black Hills. In addition, tribal members want to secure and maintain the quality of the environment in the Black Hills and other sacred sites in South Dakota. They are protesting the building of roads and the clear-cutting of forests. They consider it their sacred obligation to protect these sites because of their important spiritual meaning. And they recognize the critical role these places can play in protecting resources for future generations.

In addition to attracting industry and jobs, plains tribes, including the Tetons, have embarked on the development of businesses that will generate tourism. Members of the Rosebud and Pine Ridge Reservations are opening bed-and-breakfast lodgings and camping facilities that will appeal to "ecotourists." The region where the reservations are located is an area where tourism is growing rapidly. The area appeals particularly to tourists from North America and Europe who are concerned about environmental and cultural issues and who are interested in understanding the history and heritage of the continent.

In conjunction with ecotourism projects, the Cheyenne River Sioux have plans to turn some of their land into a tribal park. They are restoring and protecting the ecological purity of the prairie lands that have been their home for many centuries. These efforts are being applauded by conservation groups throughout the country. In the words of Stephen Torbit, director of the National Wildlife Federation's Rocky Mountain National Resource Center: "The Indians are light-years ahead of the rest of our society in seeing the importance of restoring these prairies. The rest of us have forgotten that the buffalos are wildlife that belong there, like the elk, the eagle, and the wild horses. They're the only group that after all these years has remembered these are animals that should be respected, and allowed to roam wild and free."

Despite their considerable innovative efforts to revitalize their economies, Lakota communities are facing difficulties due to revisions in federal welfare requirements enacted by Congress in 1996. Congressional legislation now requires that welfare programs eliminate payments to people who have been on the welfare rolls for specific lengths of time, usually five years. When welfare payments come to an end for individuals on Teton reservations, economic conditions will likely worsen because few jobs are available in or near their communities.

Job opportunities and economic conditions are poor in most rural regions of the United States but they are particularly inadequate on Indian reservations. For example, between 1995 and 1998, the number of families on welfare in South Dakota declined overall but few Teton families have been able to leave the welfare rolls. In 1995, Sioux families accounted for about half of all the state's welfare families, but by 1999, about sixty-six percent of families on welfare in South Dakota were Sioux.

In order to help local residents, several tribal colleges located on Lakota reservations have expanded high school equivalency services as well as job training programs. However, these programs also face difficulties because federal laws limit the amount of time a welfare recipient may be enrolled in college to one year. This restriction creates a problem because academic and job-training programs usually last a minimum of two years.

Another source of revenue has been generated by the Prairie Winds Casino. Built in 1994, the casino is located on the Pine Ridge Reservation. Although some reservation residents disapprove of gambling and think the tribe should find other ways to make money, the casino has become a leading place of employment among the Teton Sioux. With a steady stream of mainly non-Indian customers, the casino also generates a great deal of revenue that can be used for improvements on the reservation. In the fall of 2003, the tribe announced plans to build a second gaming facility to help increase economic development and provide additional jobs for Teton Sioux workers.

Even though the people face many economic problems, the population at the Teton reservations in South Dakota is steadily increasing. According to the 2000 U.S. Census Bureau, the number of residents on the five reservations were as follows:

Reservation	Total Population	Number of Native People	Percent of Native People
Pine Ridge	15,507	14,295	92.2%
Rosebud	10,469	9,040	86.4%
Cheyenne River	8,470	6,249	73.8%
Standing Rock	4,206	2,543	60.5%
Lower Brulé	1,353	1,237	91.4%

As can be seen from this list, the percentage of Lakota living on their reservations varies from community to community. At Pine Ridge and Lower Brulé—coincidentally the largest and the smallest of the reservations—more than ninety percent of the residents are Sioux. However, at Standing Rock, only about sixty percent are Natives. On all of the reservations, nearly all non-Native residents are white. Most of these non-Natives are farmers or ranchers who rent land from members of the tribes.

Additional data collected by the Census Bureau reveal that the Sioux's median age was relatively young:

Reservation	Average Age
Pine Ridge	20.6 years
Rosebud	21.5 years
Lower Brulé	21.8 years
Cheyenne River	25.7 years
Standing Rock	28.3 years

When compared to the rest of the population of the United States, these figures reveal that the median age of the Lakotas is significantly lower than the national median age, which is thirty-five years.

It is interesting to note that the reservation with the highest median age, Standing Rock, at 28.3 years, is also the reservation with the lowest percentage of Native residents. This is probably not a coincidence because American Indians tend to have higher fertility rates than whites. High fertility rates mean relatively large numbers of children per family. And, of course, large numbers of children lead to a drop in the median age of a community.

In addition, high fertility rates have an obvious effect on average family size. The figures for average number of family members for the Sioux reservations were as follows:

Reservation	Persons per Family
Pine Ridge	4.71
Lower Brulé	4.20
Rosebud	4.15
Standing Rock	3.81
Cheyenne River	3.71

In the United States, the median family size is 2.61 persons. Comparing the Lakota communities with the U.S. average indicates that Lakota families are significantly larger than most American families.

The figures for Lakota family size also reveal that the three reservations with the largest percentage of Sioux residents (Pine Ridge, Rosebud, and Lower Brulé) have the largest average family size, while the two reservations with the lowest percentages of Sioux residents (Cheyenne River and Standing Rock) have the smallest average family size.

Data collected during the 2000 U.S. Census Bureau on income and employment point to the difficult economic situation on the reservations. On all the reservations, median family incomes and per-capita incomes are much lower than national or state averages. The figures for the Lakota communities were as follows:

Reservation	Median Family Income	Per-Capita Income
Standing Rock	$23,861	$8,636
Cheyenne River	$22,917	$8,710
Pine Ridge	$20,449	$6,128
Lower Brulé	$20,263	$7,020
Rosebud	$18,673	$7,279

These figures compare unfavorably to averages for the state of South Dakota and for the United States:

	Median Family Income	Per-Capita Income
South Dakota	$31,354	$23,715
United States	$46,737	$27,203

The relatively low levels of family and per-capita income on the reservations are obviously reflected in relatively high rates of poverty:

Reservation	Percent of Families Below Poverty	Percent of Individuals Below Poverty
Pine Ridge	46.4%	53.5%
Rosebud	45.9%	50.5%
Lower Brulé	45.3%	48.3%
Cheyenne River	34.5%	38.5%
Standing Rock	32.6%	40.8%

Again, these figures compare unfavorably to poverty rates in both South Dakota and in the United States. In South Dakota, 10.8 percent of the residents were living in poverty while nationally, 12.7 percent were poor. The figures for the Lakota reservations are therefore about four times the South Dakota and national averages.

For the Lakota reservations, the statistics on both income and poverty status show an interesting trend. The three reservations with the highest percentage of Native residents (Pine Ridge, Rosebud, and Lower Brulé) have the lowest incomes and the highest poverty rates. In contrast, the two reservations with the lowest percentage of Native residents (Cheyenne River and Standing Rock) have slightly higher incomes and lower rates of poverty.

Information about employment is consistent with the data reporting income and poverty rates. Although rates of unemployment are relatively high on all reservations, they are highest in the communities with a greater percentage of Native residents:

Reservation	Percent Employed	Percent Unemployed	Percent Not in Labor Force
Pine Ridge	34.3%	16.9%	48.8%
Lower Brulé	43.5%	16.9%	39%
Rosebud	46.1%	11.6%	42.3%
Cheyenne River	48.2%	8.6%	43.1%
Standing Rock	44.6%	6.7%	48.7%

And once again, employment data for Lakota reservations demonstrate greater hardship than in other South Dakota communities and in the nation as a whole. The comparable figures for South Dakota and the United States were as follows:

	Percent Employed	Percent Unemployed	Percent Not in Labor Force
South Dakota	71.1%	2.9%	26%
United States	67.1%	4.2%	32.9%

These figures reveal that most of the residents of South Dakota are doing better than the national averages. This fact makes the high rates of unemployment on the Sioux reservations stand out in even sharper contrast with their fellow South Dakotans. Indeed, all the statistics on income, poverty, and employment reveal more economic problems on the Lakota reservations than experienced by other residents of South Dakota or the nation.

In addition to economic problems, Lakota people are concerned about issues from their past that continue to have relevance today. The tragic events of the massacre at Wounded Knee in 1890 remain deeply meaningful to the Sioux. In an act of commemoration and unity, some four hundred Lakotas participated in a prayer ritual to mark the one-hundredth anniversary of the massacre. The ceremony was held on December 29, 1990. It was dedicated to the memory of the victims of Wounded Knee and was performed at the site where their mass grave is located. More than two hundred participants rode on horseback to retrace the 220-mile path their ancestors had taken one hundred years before. Commenting on the events, spiritual leader Arvol Looking Horse said, "The ride was for unity and peace . . . an effort to mend the sacred hoop and bring our people back together."

The memory and legacy of the great Lakota leader, Crazy Horse, is being championed by a group of his descendants. Along with their supporters, members of the family have formed The Crazy Horse Defense Project, an organization created in 1993 that seeks to protect his name. Members of the committee also want to educate the American public about misuses of Indian names and symbols. This misuse occurs frequently in advertising and in the names of products and sports teams. Many Native Americans object to the practice of giving Indian names to teams and commercial goods because they believe it demeans and trivializes Native people and their heritage. In particular, the Crazy Horse Defense Project has filed a legal suit against the clothing manufacturer, Liz Claiborne, Inc., in an attempt to stop the company from marketing its Crazy Horse line of merchandise. They are also suing the Hornell Brewing Company to stop them from selling a beer product marketed as "The Original Crazy Horse Malt Liquor." Both suits are pending in federal court. (For additional information on this organization, enter "Crazy Horse Defense Project" into any search engine and browse the many sites listed.)

Demonstrators rally in front of the U.S. Court of Appeals in Denver, Colorado, to demand the release of Leonard Peltier in August 2003. Though federal guidelines call for prisoners who have been convicted of murder to be considered for parole after serving two hundred months of their sentence, Peltier will not be granted parole until 2008, despite serving more than four hundred months of his sentence.

In another critical matter, there are continuing efforts to seek the release of political prisoner Leonard Peltier. Peltier was accused and convicted of murdering two FBI agents on the Pine Ridge Reservation in 1975. Peltier has repeatedly requested a new trial on the charges, but his appeals have been turned down even though the main witness against him at the trial, a Sioux woman named Myrtle Poor Bear, later recanted her original testimony that she saw Peltier shoot the agents. During the 1990s, efforts were directed at convincing then-President Bill Clinton to grant executive clemency to Peltier. Shortly before President Clinton left office in 2001, representatives of the Department of Justice told Peltier's lawyers that the executive clemency decree was likely. However, Clinton ultimately declined to offer clemency.

Peltier's request for a parole hearing has also been denied. The denial was made on the grounds that Peltier has not shown remorse for killing the two FBI officers. This is a strange ruling because Peltier has consistently proclaimed his innocence. Since he denies having committed the crime, he obviously cannot show remorse. The U.S. Parole Commission told Peltier that it will not consider his request for parole until 2008. According to his lawyers, federal guidelines call for prisoners convicted of murder to serve two hundred months before being considered for parole but, by 2008, Peltier will have served more than four hundred months—double the federal guideline period. Peltier's lawyers have appealed to the federal courts for an earlier parole hearing date.

Despite their very real and pressing economic problems, members of the Teton tribe maintain their sense of community through the continuation of traditional rituals and the transmission of sacred knowledge. Elders in the communities instruct children through storytelling and through example.

Educational attainment for residents of the Sioux reservations is about average for Native Americans:

Reservation	Percent High School Graduate	Percent Bachelor's Degree or Higher
Standing Rock	76.1%	11.2%
Lower Brulé	75.9%	8.8%
Cheyenne River	75.6%	12.2%
Rosebud	73%	10.9%
Pine Ridge	68.8%	11.1%

Beginning in the early 1900s, when non-Native educational institutions attempted to assimilate American Indian students, tribal colleges were created as a way to uphold the cultural traditions of Native Americans. Oglala Lakota College, which has locations throughout South Dakota, is one example of such an institution. Chartered in 1971 as the Lakota Higher Education Center, the then-non-accredited institution used educators from Black Hills State College, South Dakota State, and the University of South Dakota to teach the same courses that were offered at those schools. In 1983, the college earned accreditation from the North Central Association and began offering bachelor's and associate degrees in such fields as elementary education and nursing. The college, which changed its name to Oglala Lakota College after it received accreditation, now offers bachelor's degrees in Lakota Studies, Human Services, and Applied Sciences, and a Master's in Tribal Leadership.

In addition to Oglala Lakota College, the practice of Lakota customs is also maintained at home, in schools, at ceremonies, and in public meetings and gatherings. According to census data from 2000, the following percentages of reservation residents speak Lakota:

Reservation	English Only	Lakota
Pine Ridge	74.3%	25.7%
Rosebud	77.6%	22.4%
Cheyenne River	81.6%	18.4%
Standing Rock	84.8%	15.2%
Lower Brulé	89.7%	10.3%

These figures are interesting because they vary according to the composition and size of the Native communities on the reservations. Pine Ridge and Rosebud are the largest reservations and rank first and third in the percentage of Native residents. They also have the largest percentages of speakers of Lakota. These facts indicate that, in order to maintain and continue speaking Native languages, a large community of Native people who interact often is a significant, possibly necessary, condition.

Educators and residents of the reservations are making concerted efforts to maintain and expand the use of Lakota. They have formed the Lakota Language Consortium to develop curricula and methods of teaching Lakota in elementary and secondary schools as well as in tribal colleges on or near the reservations. Many of the participating teachers are tribal elders whose advanced age makes it critical to train other qualified teachers who will be able to carry on the tradition after the elders are gone.

According to Leonard Little Finger, a teacher at Loneman School on the Pine Ridge Reservation, there is a danger that the language could disappear in about ten years: "In 1975, ninety percent of the students at Loneman School spoke Lakota. Now only three percent of the kindergarten students speak the language . . . We must revive the language to understand the culture and be able to spread and understand who we are."

Lakota teachers are also experimenting with computer technology. Computer programs for language teaching make it possible for students to hear the words and learn them in an interactive process.

Many residents understand the importance of their language as a means of expressing their values and culture. They see the loss of their language as yet another harmful effect of domination by American culture. In the words of Jesse Taken Alive, a member of the Standing Rock Tribal Council: "In Lakota we accept things and then understand them. In today's society we are not understood and not accepted. We see people use our language for money, and we are victims of linguistic racism. It turns people into objects; Crazy Horse Malt Liquor, the Fighting Sioux, for example, it's a form of conquering."

Residents of the Teton reservations continue to balance the changes brought about by their circumstances with the valued traditions of their heritage. The communities survive and provide social support and nurturance for their members. Many people who have left their home reservations, now living either in nearby towns and cities or in distant places throughout the United States, maintain strong ties to their families. They return as often as possible to visit and participate in family and community events.

Bonds among the Tetons remain strong. Although divided by territory, and sometimes by attitudes and politics, the Tetons remain convinced that they must work together in order to achieve common goals and to create a setting of harmony and prosperity for themselves and their descendants. Such was the wish of the Teton centuries ago, and such is the hope of the people today.

The Teton Sioux at a Glance

Tribe	Teton Lakota
Culture Area	Northern Plains of the United States
Geography	Minnesota, North and South Dakota, Nebraska, and Wyoming
Linguistic Family	Siouan
Current Population (2000)	Approximately 40,000 on reservations in South Dakota
First European Contact	Jacques Marquette, French, 1674
Federal Status	Tribal reservations in South Dakota: Cheyenne River, Lower Brulé, Pine Ridge, Rosebud, Standing Rock

1674	French Jesuit Jacques Marquette first makes contact with the Lakotas.
1682	French trader Pierre Le Sueur visits the Lakotas.
1695	Le Sueur brings several Teton representatives to visit traders at Montreal.
1727–1737	French missionaries work among the Lakotas.
c. 1750	Tetons cross the Missouri River and head west into the Great Plains.
1763	After the French are expelled from the East in wake of French and Indian War, trade increases between Tetons and Europeans.
c. 1765	Teton Sioux reach the Black Hills.
1805	Meriwether Lewis and William Clark describe the Lakotas as the dominant power along the Missouri River.
1816	First treaty of friendship signed between the United States and the Lakotas.
1820s	Protestant missionaries from the United Foreign Mission Society set up missions among the Lakotas.
1824	Bureau of Indian Affairs established.
1825	Another treaty of friendship is signed by the United States and the Lakotas.
1834	Rocky Mountain Fur Company builds a trading post in Teton territory on the North Platte River in what is now Wyoming; Presbyterian missionaries make contact with the Lakotas.
1837	The peoples of the Great Plains suffer from a devastating smallpox epidemic; in the Treaty of 1837, the Lakotas agree to cede to the United States all the lands they had once possessed east of the Mississippi River.
1848	Gold is discovered in California, sparking a mass wave of migration to the West.
1850s–1860s	Roman Catholic missionaries make contact with the Lakotas; warfare intensifies on the Great Plains as white settlers cross Indian territory.

1851   A treaty signed by the Lakotas and the United States marks the end of treaties of friendship and the start of massive losses of Lakota land to white settlement; in the Fort Laramie Treaty, the Lakotas are forced to give up much of their land in present-day South Dakota.

1860s–1870s   Efforts to kill the buffalo intensify.

1861–1865   American Civil War is fought.

1868   In a treaty signed at Fort Laramie, the Tetons give to the United States much of the remaining land they possess in South Dakota, keeping for themselves the area between the Missouri River and the western part of South Dakota.

1871   Teton leader Red Cloud visits New York City to give a speech at the Cooper Institute.

1874   Gold is discovered in the Black Hills of South Dakota, leading the U.S. government to deny Teton rights to their lands there.

1876   Many Tetons assist the Cheyennes when they are attacked by the U.S. Army; in March, the U.S. government orders the cavalry to round up all Lakotas and force them onto their reservations; in June, Lieutenant Colonel George Armstrong Custer and his U.S. troops are massacred by Teton warriors at the Battle of the Little Bighorn.

1877   When the Tetons refuse to sell any more land, the U.S. government ignores the Treaty of 1868 and seizes the Black Hills; Teton leader Crazy Horse is arrested and killed by U.S. forces.

1881   Teton leader Sitting Bull surrenders to U.S. authorities.

1887   General Allotment Act (also called the Dawes Act) is passed by Congress; intended to break up the reservations and parcel out smaller blocks of land to individual Indians.

1889   The Great Sioux Reservation is split into five smaller reservations; Congress passes the Sioux Act, intended to encourage the Tetons to accept land allotments; Wovoka (also known as Jack Wilson) popularizes the Ghost Dance religion.

1890   President Benjamin Harrison issues orders to prevent any performance of the Ghost Dance; on November 20, U.S. troops surround the Pine Ridge and Rosebud Reservations; in December, Sitting Bull is killed by troops; on December 29, more than three hundred Tetons are killed at Wounded Knee, South Dakota.

1891   Kicking Bear, the last Teton chief to surrender to authorities, turns himself in to U.S. forces.

1898   Congress passes the Curtis Act, ending Indian land tenure.

1917   United States enters World War I.

1924   The U.S. government grants citizenship to all Native Americans.

1928   Meriam Report on the state of Indian reservations is issued.

1934   Congress passes the Indian Reorganization Act, allowing for limited tribal self-government.

1935   The Teton reservations set up tribal councils and write constitutions.

1950s   U.S. government institutes a policy aimed at encouraging Indians to leave reservations and move to urban areas.

1960s   President Lyndon Johnson's Great Society program provides new jobs on Teton reservations.

1968   Russell Means, Dennis Banks, and Vernon and Clyde Bellecourt found the American Indian Movement (AIM).

1969   More than one hundred American Indians from all over the United States take over Alcatraz Island, claiming it as Indian territory.

1972   AIM members hold a demonstration called the Trail of Broken Treaties to show how the U.S. government has historically failed to live up to its treaty promises with Indians; Raymond Yellow Thunder, an Oglala man from Pine Ridge, is murdered; the Oglala Sioux Civil Rights Organization is founded at Pine Ridge; Gerald One Feather and Richard Wilson compete in a bitter campaign for president of the tribal council at Pine Ridge; Wilson wins and tries to suppress opposition.

1973   Some of Wilson's opponents form the Inter-District Council of the Oglala Sioux file impeachment proceedings against Wilson who responds by calling in U.S. forces to keep the peace; AIM members go to Wounded Knee to bring publicity to the Teton people's problems.

1974   Tetons awarded $17.5 million to make up for land they lost in the Black Hills.

1975   Leonard Peltier is arrested for the murder of two FBI agents; he remains in prison (many people say unjustly) to this day.

1978   Congress passes the American Indian Religious Freedom Act.

1980   Tetons awarded $105 million for lost lands in a verdict upheld by the U.S. Supreme Court.

1987   U.S. Supreme Court rules that if a state permits any type of gambling, then Indian casinos there are legal; the following year Congress passes the Indian Gaming Regulatory Act, requiring reservations to negotiate with states in order to have certain types of casino operations.

1993   The Crazy Horse Defense Project is formed to protect the name of the nineteenth-century leader and to ensure that mascots and other symbols are used with respect for Native Americans.

1994   Prairie Winds Casino opens at the Pine Ridge Reservation.

2001   President Bill Clinton declines to extend amnesty to Leonard Peltier.

2003   Tetons announce plans to build another gaming facility.

agent—A person appointed by the Bureau of Indian Affairs to supervise U.S. government programs on a reservation and/or in a specific region.

American Indian Movement (AIM)—Native rights organization, founded in 1968, that used militant tactics to draw attention to the adverse conditions facing Native Americans.

annuity—Money or goods paid yearly or at a regular interval.

band—A loosely organized group of people who are bound together by the need for food and defense, by family ties, and/or by other common interests.

bilateral descent—Kinship traced through both the mother's and the father's families.

breechcloth—A strip of animal skin or cloth that is drawn between the legs and hung from a belt tied around the waist.

Bureau of Indian Affairs (BIA)—A federal government agency now part of the Department of the Interior. Originally intended to manage trade and other relations with Indians, the BIA now seeks to develop and implement programs that encourage Indians to manage their own affairs and to improve their educational opportunities and general social and economic well-being.

counting coup—System of ranking acts of bravery in war, with the highest honor going to warriors who attacked an enemy at close contact.

culture—The learned behavior of humans; nonbiological, socially taught activities; the way of life of a group of people.

Dawes Act—The 1887 federal law, also known as the General Allotment Act, that called for dividing reservation land into small parcels assigned to individual families. This policy undermined the traditional Native way of life.

dialect—A regional variant of a particular language with unique elements of grammar, pronunciation, and vocabulary.

Ghost Dance religion—A religion started in 1889 that prophesied the end of the world, followed by a return to traditional Native American life. Believers participated in ceremonies and dances of hope and celebration, which were eventually banned by the U.S. government.

Heyoka—A prestigious Teton social group whose members were called by spirit visions and had to do everything in reverse.

Indian Reorganization Act (IRA)—The 1934 federal law that ended the policy of allotting plots of land to individuals and encouraged the development of reservation communities. The act also provided for the creation of autonomous tribal governments.

nomadic—Moving from place to place, often relying on the season or food supply, and establishing only temporary camps.

peace chief—An older man who was respected for his intelligence, compassion, and skill in hunting and healing.

reservation—A tract of land retained by Indians for their own occupation and use.

roach—A young man's hairstyle in which the sides of the head are shaved, with only the hair in the center allowed to grow.

Sun Dance—A sacred ritual performed every summer in which the Tetons give thanks for good fortune by performing different acts. In the most dramatic facet of the ritual, men pierce their flesh and dance around a pole until they are torn free.

sweat bath—A ritual purification, considered sacred by the Tetons, that prepares people to face the world of supernatural beings.

tipi—An easily transportable, cone-shaped home, rounded at the base and tapered to an open smoke hole at the top, that is made of buffalo hides and wooden poles.

treaty—A contract negotiated between sovereign nations. Treaties between the U.S. government and the Indian tribes dealt with the cessation of military action, the surrender of political independence, the establishment of boundaries, terms of land sales, and related matters.

tribe—A society consisting of several or many separate communities united by kinship, culture, language, and other social institutions; including clans, religious organizations, and warrior societies.

Vision Quest—A sacred ritual in which a person, spiritually purified through a fast and a sweat bath, went off alone for four days of fasting and praying in order to receive visions from a supernatural spirit who would act as a personal guardian.

war chief—A younger man who, while brave and daring in leading men in warfare, was under the authority of the older peace chiefs.

Primary Sources

Brown, Joseph Epes, ed. *The Sacred Pipe: Black Elk's Account of the Seven Rites of the Oglala Sioux: Black Elk, Holy Man of the Oglala.* Norman, Okla.: University of Oklahoma Press, 1997.

Crow Dog, Mary. *Lakota Woman.* New York: Perennial, 1994.

Deloria, Vine, Jr. *Behind the Trail of Broken Treaties.* New York: Dell, 1974.

———. *Custer Died for Your Sins.* New York: Avon Books, 1969.

Greene, Jerome A. *Lakota and Cheyenne: Indian Views of the Great Sioux War, 1876–1877.* Norman, Okla.: University of Oklahoma Press, 2003.

Grobsmith, Elizabeth. *Lakota of the Rosebud: A Contemporary Ethnography.* New York: Holt, Rinehart & Winston, 1981.

Hull, Michael. *Sun Dancing: A Spiritual Journey on the Red Road.* Rochester, Vt.: Inner Traditions International Ltd., 2000.

Josephy, Alvin M., Jr. "Crazy Horse." In *The Patriot Chiefs: A Chronicle of American Indian Resistance.* New York: Viking Books, 1958.

Kehoe, Alice. *The Ghost Dance: Ethnohistory and Revitalization.* New York: Holt, Rinehart & Winston, 1989.

Mooney, James. *The Ghost Dance Religion and the Sioux Outbreak of 1890.* Chicago: University of Chicago Press, 1965.

Neihardt, John. *Black Elk Speaks: Being the Life Story of a Holy Man of the Oglala Sioux.* Lincoln, Nebr.: University of Nebraska Press, 1961.

Powers, William. *Oglala Religion.* Norman, Okla.: University of Oklahoma Press, 1985.

Price, John. *Native Studies: American and Canadian Indians.* Toronto: McGraw-Hill/Ryerson, 1978.

Spencer, Robert F., Theodore Stern, and Kenneth Stewart. *The Native Americans: Ethnology and Backgrounds of the Native American Indians.* New York: Macmillan, 1981.

Standing Bear, Luther. *My Indian Boyhood.* Lincoln, Nebr.: University of Nebraska Press, 1988.

———. *My People, the Sioux.* Lincoln, Nebr.: University of Nebraska Press, 1975.

Sword, Finger, One-Starr, and Tyon, through J.R. Walker. "Oglala Metaphysics." In *Teachings from the American Earth: Indian Religion & Philosophy*, ed. by Dennis Tedlock and Barbara Tedlock. New York: Liveright, 1988.

Talbot, Steve. *Roots of Oppression.* New York: International, 1981.

Secondary Sources

Bucko, Raymond A. *The Lakota Ritual of the Sweat Lodge: History and Contemporary Practice.* Lincoln, Nebr.: University of Nebraska Press, 1999.

Crow Dog, Leonard. *Crow Dog: Four Generations of Sioux Medicine Men.* New York: Perennial, 1996.

Erdoes, Richard. *Lame Deer: Seeker of Visions.* New York: Simon & Schuster, 1994.

Gonzalez, Mario, and Elizabeth Cook-Lynn. *The Politics of Hallowed Ground: Wounded Knee and the Struggle for Indian Sovereignty.* Champaign, Ill.: University of Illinois Press, 1999.

Marshall, Joseph III. *Lakota Way: Stories & Lessons for Living.* New York: Viking Press, 2001.

Matthiessen, Peter. *In the Spirit of Crazy Horse.* New York: Penguin USA, 1992.

Michno, Gregory F. *Lakota Noon: The Indian Narrative of Custer's Defeat.* Missoula, Mont.: Mountain Press Publishing Company, 1997.

Websites

American Indians
http://www.americanindians.com/Sioux.htm

Cheyenne River Sioux Tribe
http://www.sioux.org

History Channel Exhibits: The Great Sioux Nation of the Nineteenth Century
http://www.historychannel.com/exhibits/ sioux/chrono.html

Pine Ridge Reservation
http://www.pineridgerez.net/index.php

Rosebud Reservation
http://tradecorridor.com/rosebud

South Dakota State Historical Society (Lower Brulé Reservation)
http://www.sdhistory.org/arc/iap/ arc_iap21.htm

Standing Rock Reservation
http://www.standingrock.org

Teton Sioux Indians
http://www.pbs.org/lewisandclark/ native/idx_tet.html

The Teton Sioux (Lakota)
http://www.humboldt.edu/~wrd1/ legacyte.htm

page:

4: Minnesota Historical Society
6: South Dakota State Archives
10: Walters Art Gallery
20: New York Public Library,
    Special Collections
29: © Francis G. Mayer/CORBIS
36: Library of Congress,
    LC-USZ62-11568
39: © CORBIS
47: Library of Congress
53: © Smithsonian Institution
58: © CORBIS
64: © Bob Rowan; Progressive Image/
    CORBIS
70: © Bettmann/CORBIS
77: Associated Press, AP/
    Cliff Schiappa

81: Associated Press, AP/
    Ann Heisenfelt
94: Associated Press, AP/
    Jack Dempsey
A: © Werner Forman/
    Art Resource, NY
B: © Werner Forman/
    Art Resource, NY
C: © Werner Forman/
    Art Resource, NY
D: © Richard A. Cooke/CORBIS
E: © Werner Forman/
    Art Resource, NY
F: © Werner Forman/
    Art Resource, NY
G: © Christie's Images/CORBIS
H: © Christie's Images/CORBIS

Cover: © Werner Forman/Art Resource, NY

Nancy Bonvillain, Ph.D., is currently a visiting faculty member in the summer session at Columbia University and teaches anthropology and linguistics at Simon's Rock College of Bard in Great Barrington, Massachusetts. She has written more than a dozen books including volumes in Chelsea House's INDIANS OF NORTH AMERICA series (*The Huron, Mohawk, Hopi, Teton Sioux, Haida, Sac and Fox, Inuit, Zuni, Santee Sioux, Native American Religion* and *Native American Medicine*). And she has written two volumes of Native American biographies, *Hiawatha* and *Black Hawk*, in the NORTH AMERICAN INDIANS OF ACHIEVEMENT series.

Dr. Bonvillain's concentrations within the field have been in Native American studies and in linguistics. She has carried out fieldwork in the Navajo Nation in Arizona and the Akwesasne Mohawk Reserve in Ontario/Quebec and New York. Her dissertation was a study of the Mohawk language as spoken at the Akwesasne Reserve. She has also prepared a Mohawk/English dictionary and book of conversations for use at the schools on the reserve.

Ada E. Deer is the director of the American Indian Studies program at the University of Wisconsin-Madison. She was the first woman to serve as chair of her tribe, the Menominee Nation, the first woman to head the Bureau of Indian Affairs in the U.S. Department of the Interior, and the first American Indian woman to run for Congress and secretary of state of Wisconsin. Deer has also chaired the Native American Rights Fund, coordinated workshops to train American Indian women as leaders, and championed Indian participation in the Peace Corps. She holds degrees in social work from Wisconsin and Columbia.